INVENTOR'S

Patent, Protect, Produce And Profit
From Your Ideas and Inventions
Yourself!

By
Victor N. Vic-Vincent

Copy Editors
Timothy Jordan
Kaitlyn Loftus

Cover Design
Steven J. Smith

INVENTORS!

Patent, Protect, Produce and Profit From Your Ideas and Inventions Yourself!

By Victor N. Vic-Vincent

Published by:

Vic-Vincent Publishing Company
362 Gulf Breeze Parkway #151
Gulf Breeze, Florida 32561 U.S.A.

Library of Congress Control Number: 2005922387
ISBN-13: 978-09646817-1-2
ISBN-10: 0-9646817-1-4

Caution:
The editor has used the most up-to-date information available in this book. However, laws, regulations and prices are subject to change. Before using this information be sure to check the validity of the information in question with the correct agency or office listed throughout this book.

TABLE OF CONTENTS

 # *Introduction*

My name is Vic-Vincent. I am an entrepreneur. I enjoy the life I live and the attention I get from being a self-made entrepreneur. I can relate to all the hardships you have endured or will endure. I am not going to give you a speech on how you can become a millionaire. If I did, it would be on "How to get people to believe anything you tell them and sell them some useless marketing brochures, promotional material and tapes." That's what all these so called marketing gurus are doing. I get tired of reading, hearing, and watching seminars about wealthy people on TV talk about how you too can be just like them. If they are so successful and wealthy, why are they giving seminars? Why aren't they in Hawaii, basking in the sun, being waited on hand and foot, just like you know we would be doing if we became rich?

I also do not like to read or hear about these entrepreneurs who made 100 million dollars last year. No kidding! They probably started with 99 million dollars that their rich parents gave them. Are these people really entrepreneurs? Can you relate to them? I can't! If you can't, then this book is for you. I designed it so someone can get started right away with his or her ideas or creations on the lowest budget possible. This book cost me much less to pre-publish on my own then what the original publisher quoted me, and that's more proof that I know how to create ideas on a budget. By myself! I hope I can help you create one of your ideas, too. That's why I wrote this book, so those with little or no knowledge can turn their dreams and ideas into reality from what I have learned. I have been successful in creating products and businesses throughout my life, maybe not ultra-profitable businesses or products, but I never consider any venture a failure, and neither should you.

Introduction

The only failure is in never trying! I have created many products on the market, and I have started many businesses from my ideas. I created and started most of these products and ventures on my own, with no help from anyone and with no degree in marketing. I have also been involved in the selling and marketing of products by numerous other companies. This book is designed so you too can create your ideas and businesses on your own, just as I have. I'll teach you how to find your own manufacturers, buyers, sellers, and even legal representatives. Don't get conned by those idea and invention companies who say they will do all these things for you. You can do it yourself and save hundreds of dollars, maybe even thousands, if your product becomes a hit. These companies are just preying off your inexperience. Doing it yourself is not that hard, and believe me, it's so simple to produce your own inventions that I know your going to say "Why didn't I think of that!"

And after reading this book you will be thinking of that! (Producing your inventions, on your own). I have been confronted many times by people who while trying to produce their invention have been deceived by some person or company designed to help them with their invention. The bottom line was the only thing they were helping them with was shrinking their bank accounts. I have even talked to some who have been harmed by lawyers, mostly because the lawyer wasn't an expert in the field of copyrights, trademarks, or patents, and even some who were coerced by attorneys into seeking patents not needed for their specific product. I hope that this hasn't happened to you and won't after reading this book, but if it has happened, don't be discouraged. There are people out there who really will help you with your ideas or creations. It's just a matter of time until you run across someone who has the same interests as you, but that person isn't going to come knocking on your door; you must go knocking on his or hers. Keep knocking and knocking and one day the right person will answer.

Introduction

There are many ways to find legitimate companies, but you must not accept the first "we help inventors ad" you read, or hear on the radio. Don't take the advice of the TV talk show personalities that say "my company can do the work for you." You can do it yourself! You must do the research on several different companies and manufacturers before you decide to use their services. The biggest complaint I hear from inventors is that they are getting swindled by companies who advertise for creators of new products. For the most part, these companies are just making money from your laziness. They survive on your passive behavior. These invention groups will also keep you hooked as long as possible. Sometimes, they even have you sign yearly or even lifetime contracts. What this does is keep you from promoting your own invention because if you find someone that's interested in your idea, you are still liable to the company who has you under contract. Of the many idea/invention companies that have inventors' contracts, only a few out of thousands of inventors have ever made a profit!

These invention companies also have lawyers either within their company or on retainer, and, anything extra they tell you that you need, like patents, et cetera, you can be sure they have a markup to include those fees. So, not only do they make money from you for their services, but anything else they do will also cost you more than if you did it yourself because most of these things that you are paying someone else to do may just be a simple phone call, a phone call that could save you hundreds of dollars. Every year thousands of independent inventor's, like yourself, are targeted by unscrupulous invention promotion, marketing and licensing firms. You need to do your own ground work and learn about patents, et cetera. Don't rely on other people to do the work for you because they won't have the same energy you have. It's your product; make it work yourself! Learn to find out how to contact companies who may be interested in your ideas. Pick up a book. Pick up a phone.

Introduction

It's just a matter of knowing who to call and how to find out where these specific professionals can be located, and I'm prepared to tell you of my experiences, my failures, and my accomplishments so that you can learn from my mistakes and save time and money. You must become determined to make yourself successful. It won't be easy because if it were easy, everyone with an idea would be a millionaire. You will benefit from doing everything on your own, like learning about the market you are entering, and when you are talking to experts in the field of your creation, at least you will have some idea what they are talking about. If you have someone else doing the talking for you, you will always depend on them unless you know your business. I want you to realize you must be a part of the whole process from the start. After you have a firm grip on your product and your company, then you should delegate other duties, like sales, to other people.

Don't be afraid to make mistakes. If you do not make any mistakes, then you are not trying hard enough. I still stutter to this day when I get on the phone to make a sales pitch because I'm nervous, but nervous or not, someone has to do it, and I want that someone to be me. I don't want to have to rely on someone else and neither should you! Take control! Make your product and yourself famous. Make everyone around you jealous of your success. Don't rely on anyone or any company to do what you can do yourself. This book is designed for amateur entrepreneurs, but even professionals can relate and even learn something. I know. I learn from successful and unsuccessful people all the time. If I didn't, I wouldn't be writing this book, and here's another incentive piece: I didn't know anything about writing books either, but I found out from people who have. I found editors, copy editors, printers, publishing companies, et cetera, and I accomplished this all on my own, and you can too. I paid no one to do the research for me; I operated everything on a low budget just like you will have to!

Introduction

No one gave me anything. I saved. I took out loans. I negotiated prices. I borrowed from people. I sold things I owned to produce my products and start my businesses. I hope you never have to go that far, but many entrepreneurs do. They sacrifice for what they believe in. They are determined to become successful on their own. That's why you don't need anyone or any company taking advantage of you or your money. You are going to have a tough enough time as it is. This tough time does not mean quit your job to work on your idea…. I repeat; DO NOT QUIT YOUR JOB! I have seen too many entrepreneurs get caught up in the exhilaration of creating their dream, up and leave their job, just to find out they can not continue that dream because their cash flow dried up. Continue working and marketing your creation until you are satisfied you can live comfortably on what you make. You are going to have to work really hard.

No matter how many supportive non-fiction titles you read, it all comes down to your determination. I am no one special; I'm an average person. I just have a desire to succeed, just like you. I have other entrepreneurial stories in this book to show you that you are not alone. Many behind you and many in front of you have and will go through the same things you have and will go through. It will be the determination of that person that makes him or her successful. I hope that this written text will help keep you from becoming a victim and if you have, how not to again! Read on, and learn how to patent, protect, produce, and profit from your own ideas, inventions and creations yourself, so you can avoid becoming the prey of someone or some company out to "help you."

HELP YOURSELF!
READ ON. IT'S TIME TO
MAKE YOUR DREAMS A REALITY!

Chapter One
The Idea

Your idea is no good if it's just an idea. You must act on it, believe in it, and create it. How many times have you heard someone say, "I have this great idea!" No one is impressed with people who talk about doing things and never accomplish them. Keep this picture in the back of your mind. (You are sitting in your rocking chair, talking to your grandchildren, telling them about this great idea you had when you were young that could have made you rich, and thinking to yourself that you should of acted on it). No one wants to hear what you could have done. They want to hear what you have done.

I know you are not that type of person, or you would not have bought this book. You just need direction and incentive, and I'm going to give you both. So, let's do it! Right now! I will show you how, and I hope one of your ideas makes you MILLIONS! Let's get started. It's your idea; get a pencil, (or coloring pencils) and a notebook. Write your idea down; draw pictures and diagrams; put down dimensions, shade in areas of importance, do whatever it takes; move your mind; think of ways to produce your idea. What am I going to use: metal, plastic, paper, or cardboard? Where will I buy this material? Where are the manufacturers? How many will I make? Whom will I sell to? Men, women, children? That's it! You're thinking now! Already your idea is becoming a reality.

Ideas

Let's go! Let's go! How much will I charge? More importantly, how much will I make? Do I need sales people? Can I produce this myself and save money? Can I sell it myself and avoid paying commissions? These are all questions that you need answers to. So get motivated and answer them. Are you feeling it now? Motivation! Inspiration! Good! Then create a working production table in your notebook to help you keep records so your answers will be in one place for easy access. While you are trying to produce this product, you can refer to this information for a quick reference. Put in as many answers to the questions we just talked about as you can. Now! Don't procrastinate! If you do not have an idea for a business or a product, don't worry. I will explain how you can get ideas for new creations or just make old ones better. Our minds are creating ideas all the time, but we don't pay attention. Start paying attention.

The idea comes to us during impromptu situations, usually during times we are already concentrating on something else, so we ignore the interruption and concentrate on what we are doing, trying not to store anything in our memory to disturb what we were already doing. I bet several times while you were watching TV, writing a letter, or even doing something at work, you came up with a great idea but couldn't remember it later. This is my greatest kept secret, and it's very simple. Just keep a pen and a piece of paper in your top pocket or your purse, somewhere that you have easy access to. Write it down, and later, when you have the time, see if it could be something of interest that you could act on. If it is not something you can utilize right now, put it away for future reference. You may never know when it might prove useful. Even though you think right now your ideas have no purpose, you don't want to be kicking yourself later when you may have a use for it, and you couldn't remember what it was. This way, all you have to remember is where it is! The best time for your mind to create these inventions is in bed while you are asleep. That's right, I said asleep.

Ideas

I lost probably my best creations and inventions when I was younger in my sleep because when I woke up, I couldn't remember what they were. So, I decided what I would do was keep a piece of paper and pencil beside my bed, so when I would dream these great things, I could wake up in the middle of the night and write them down; and this works. That's how I created the board game "BANKRUPTCY!" I was having financial troubles and I dreamed about a game in my sleep that turned an unpleasant situation into a enjoyable situation by making me laugh. I awoke in the middle of the night, went to my kitchen table and drew it all out on paper. By morning, I was through with the prototype, and, in ninety days, I had finished the whole process and had one-thousand "BANKRUPTCY!" board games completed, packaged for sale, and stacked up in my living room. What a sight!

Your car is also a great place. When you are driving and you are alone, you have plenty of time to think. So train those thoughts to create images, images of new products, inventions, even businesses. There is plenty going on around you while you are driving; maybe the radio's on, think about writing a song, making some product for driver comfort, maybe even something technological, like cruise control. It's really not that hard. Someone came up with the idea and made it a reality, and so can you. Train your brain; if you cannot think of ideas, start teaching yourself to glance around at different goods and think to yourself, "How can I make that product better?" Remember, your mind will work with or without you, so it's important to be aware that your mind is creating ideas all the time, but you don't pay attention. From now on, you will, and you will be prepared to write it down. It takes no special talent or intelligence. It just takes someone with the ability to recognize there are better ways of improving prehistoric products. All minds basically work the same; it just takes a creative person to listen. My mind amazes me, and yours will amaze you.

Ideas

When you start this creative learning process, you will find that it's like having a personal computer that you can bring up information whenever you need it; you can create it, change it, even re-arrange it, but make sure that you store it where it can be helpful to you later, like on paper in a fire proof security box! Don't rely on your memory because when it comes to storing information in our minds, it does not always come back to us as fast as we would like, and sometimes, it even loses that information and doesn't come back to us at all....LOL. (Laugh Out Loud). Keep a file with your ideas in it, or, if you have a computer, store them on your hard drive, but always make a backup. Let's talk about things that might benefit you, things that you can start creating today; some change almost every year or season.

1. Clothing
2. Computers
3. Automobiles
4. Plants & Flowers
5. Games + Gimmicks
6. Cosmetics
7._____

Again, this chapter is about showing you how you can create ideas and make products for consumer use. These are just **Einstein / Inventor** a few items you could become involved with. Ideally, we would like to create something that the general public uses every day such as toothpaste: something we use, throw away, and have to buy again. First, you must find a subject that interests you, and, if it is not one of these, use line 7 to put in your own. Let's use clothing as an example. What a great industry this is. It changes not only every year, but also every season! T-Shirts are big business. You could change the design of the T-shirts as some-one did by putting in a V-neck.

Ideas

You could create a saying that attracts everyone's attention, or you could put certain prints, like animals, cars, et cetera on them by silk screening or computer printing. Maybe even paint or tie dye them. You don't always have to do something that no one has ever done before; you just have to do it differently or find a different use for it. So, fill in your blank and start creating your idea! We are all inventors at heart, but, mostly, we invent with just our common sense; but nothing can come of nothing, so we must pursue these ideas to become an inventor. We do that by first acknowledging we have a creative idea, then creating it. This is the end result. To get to this point, we first have to do some ground work. Developing an idea is a combination of images in our mind that we have previously or presently stored in our memory. It is information we have stored on many visual items and many learned items, such as reading or hands-on experience. All of this is stored in the mind. The more we learn on a subject, the more we can visualize.

As with your present job, the more you learn, the more ways you learn how to do it better. I believe people who have different ideas all the time are not much smarter than anyone else; they just have more experiences to rely on. This gives them more images in their intellect to create from. This is what your dreams are made from: images from past and present knowledge. If our experience is drawn from one source, let's say we worked around automobiles all our life, maybe we would not conjure up a thousand different ideas, but we would conjure up a thousand ideas related to automobiles. Observe, analyze, and look at ways to change or improve things. Most ideas in the preliminary stages are not based on thought; our mind is truly analytical and observational. Observe a product and analyze how to make it better. Teach yourself to do this on as many products as you come across. Soon you will find, when you are talking with someone, listening to the radio, watching television, or even reading the paper, ideas will come to you.

Ideas

It's important that you believe your ideas are possible. Because without the possibility of believing, you will not pursue your idea. Everything is possible; by believing it's possible, your mind will continue evaluating and creating possibilities with the information you supply. Do not let negative thoughts enter your mind, and do not let negative people dissuade you. Creativeness will create feelings of euphoria. Your ideas will provide you with a sense of self-esteem, self-satisfaction, and success. All you have to do is look around. There are many things that could use changing or so many things that need to be created to make our life a little better. The opportunities are endless. Most of the time, we view these new thoughts of inventions as just that, thoughts. We find ourselves stumped by the unknown, but no longer; use your process of observing, analyzing, and gathering research to find a solution. Don't listen to those who say it can't be done. Avoid these people.

These people will only be happy if they can deter you from your goal and make you as unproductive as they are. Create a place to be creative where you can pursue your positive mental thoughts and come to a solution. Creativeness is not born in us; it's created by us. Keep an open mind, and rule out nothing in your effort to make your invention a reality. Plan your course of action, keep notes, and continually refer to them. This will keep your thought process on 24-hour alert. Your intellect will be constantly analyzing and developing your idea in your conscious and subconscious, even in your sleep. So keep gathering information for your brain, and, one day, your idea will become an invention. Avoid the same routines. Relate to people who have different interests. Go to places you would not normally go. Read articles on subjects that you would not normally read, subjects that stimulate the psyche. Read articles in fields that you would never before consider and study topics that may have value in the future such as space exploration, computer technology or bio-chemistry. You make the choice.

Ideas

Unless you develop a knack for ideas of the unusual, it's most likely all this new information will just be helpful in analyzing your interests. Say, like we discussed before, you work around automobiles or you're an auto mechanic. All these new experiences will just be helpful in creating an idea for automobiles. This new process of learning isn't to change your profession. It's to give you better insight to the ideas you already have, like space technology that is added to the auto industry. With this new knowledge, we can create a more attractive invention. Maybe a new futuristic mode of transportation can be created from our knowledge of two different fields. Aviation and Autos. Keep an open mentality, keep a diary of your thoughts, and plan your execution. Have patience, and stick to your game plan. Do not waiver, no matter how disillusioned you become. You must realize all inventors ride those highs and lows, and, without the proper mental attitude to stay on track, they would become like everyone else.

Imagination is the key. If you can imagine it, it's possible. Do not put any limits on yourself. Your imagination is endless. This thought process puts together our knowledge of the past and our forethought for the future and creates ideas. Ideas can be corrected with our thought process by visualizing these ideas over and over again, constantly improving on our creation, even before we create it. This process of imagining and creating an invention in our brain is truly remarkable, and it's something only the inventor can understand. It makes the inventor even at awe  with him or herself and gives the inventor a true sense of self-worth and accomplishment. Could you ever of imagined Disney World, the Space Shuttle, or computers like we have now? Unbelievable!

Ideas

These are truly significant creations. It's not as unbelievable as many thought! It is now a reality, a reality that is now the past. Look to the future with your thoughts, and you may even create greater things. Take your ideas and thoughts and connect them with other ideas and thoughts and produce your end result. It's almost mathematical, except we use images in our minds to create conclusions to our project. Everyone has an imagination, but what keeps us from pursuing our idea is the thought of failure. We sometimes create images that we fear. Keep your thoughts on more positive creations, creations that you can relate to. Keep your thought process on ideas that are attainable and fulfill these goals one at a time. When you spend your time imagining the goals you want out of life, your mind will create images to pursue these goals. That's the lesson. Train your thinking to keep positive images.

Almost every journalist learns the first rules of writing with the five W's. They are Who? What? When? Where? Why? Use similar words to structure your ideas especially in writing books or press releases, or use my idea process of analyzing and reanalyzing old products to make new products and come up with your own W's (your own questions) to help you get started on a motivational plan. Create your own idea process to structure steps for creative thinking. Then when you create an idea, you can mentally visualize your project and think of similarities and dissimilarities with your product and others and make corrections. Then go a little bit farther into the future with questions: What's the lifetime of your product, not only with manufacturing parts, but the lifetime of your product in relation to how long the public will enjoy it? Will it just be a fad, or will it be a product that can be used for a lifetime? Picture in your mind your idea, add, eliminate, and rearrange parts, continue this process until you have overcome your problems, then draft your design on paper. After this process is completed, begin the next process, produce your product. Create it!

Ideas

Once created, that's not the end of it. A good inventor will keep devising ways to improve it, and by improving his invention, he creates a longer life for it. Do not become discouraged; developing an idea is a learning process. You made your first step by reading this chapter, and now you should have a better understanding of how ideas are created. When you have created your idea on paper and made a prototype design, I suggest you have your product evaluated with a third party objective. A company such as, The WIN Innovation Center. WIN is an inventor/innovator assistance service that provides inventors, entrepreneurs, and product marketing/manufacturing enterprises with a honest and objective third-party analysis of the risks and potential of their ideas, inventions, and new products.

The founder of this institute has been evaluating inventions since 1974 and if you think you are going to get an evaluation recommending you great fortune, think again. In a span of eight years this company evaluated over 4,500 inventions, and in a recent sampling of 400 of those inventions only 8% were recommended for review by large national retail/reseller chains. So, plan on a straight-forward analysis. WIN is <u>not</u> associated with any invention promotion firms and provides no additional services. Although they do provide Resource Network listings, WIN receives no compensation for referrals. The cost per analysis can be found on their website **www.wini2.com**. After you or someone else has evaluated your product the next step is to protect your product from other people who might want to copy it. In the next chapter, we will discuss what avenues you must pursue to get the protection you need.

Chapter Two
Copyrights, Trademarks, and Patents

After you have created your product, this is your next stride: protecting your creation. All your creations must remain confidential. Do not even whisper your idea to anyone, and do not take someone in confidence because it will not remain confidential. It's like telling your friend a secret and telling them not to tell anyone, and the next thing you know, someone is telling you about your secret and telling you not to tell anyone! Sometimes though, we must tell someone, so in those cases, all you can do is have that person or company sign a non-disclosure (confidentiality) document on your invention.

That makes them liable if they try to recreate it, you can search for one on the internet. I found **www.lawdepot.com** easy to use and reasonably priced. They have confidentiality agreements for inventors that can be used for general purposes, but for special creations and inventions, it's best that you have a lawyer draw up a non-disclosure form that fits your needs and pertains to your specific creation. I strongly suggest you seek the counsel of a lawyer anyway because in all actuality, these forms probably have no legal standing without some sort of documentation proving that this is your creation such as a provisional patent that could be considered Patent Pending. (See Chapter Seven on Provisional Patents).

Copyrights, Trademarks, and Patents

In one such case, I created the SLIM-PATCH (a Transdermal Weight-Loss Patch) for over-the-counter sales. I contacted my attorney to protect my invention, but he informed me that this particular product could not be patented because I created no new drug, but used those already on the market. Because this product was un-patentable, all I had to do was trademark the name. I spent a few hundred dollars for his legal opinion but saved thousands in patent costs. So, I trademarked the name SLIM-PATCH, made up several prototypes, and confronted several companies on this product, but, before I showed them the prototype, I had them sign my non-disclosure agreement to protect me and my product from being counterfeited. If you sign anyone else's non-disclosure agreement on your invention, make sure you check the time limit of their non-disclosure form.

With any luck, it will be eternity, or indefinite just like yours but, if not, make sure you agree on it before you show them your product or tell them about it! (This time limit is the time you have to create and protect your product before this company can use the information you gave them and make your creation or invention themselves). So, this is where a non-disclosure agreement could prove useful, but, if you have no legal documentation of your product, a non-disclosure form may not protect you, so keep records. Believe me, I would start a business from someone who told me about an idea. It's a smart person who can capitalize on someone else's idea. Most people just talk about them anyway, and think of all the great inventions that could be lost, some that could help humanity. Say, for instance, Thomas Edison was just a talker, and he was talking about the light bulb. I would offer to help him create it, but, if he showed no interest, then I would become the inventor and create it, and I would reap all the benefits myself! I owe him nothing because he did not put forth any effort into its creation.

Copyrights, Trademarks, and Patents

He was just a talker with an idea! Well, fortunately, Thomas Edison was not just a talker, and we have many fine inventions from that man. Now, did I worry you? I hope so. Seek legal advice before you go anywhere with your idea or invention. You must take the correct legal steps to protect yourself and your product. Most people who talk about their ideas will never pursue them, and, just to show people how serious I am, when someone comes to me with an idea, I immediately tell them not to tell me about their creation, invention, or idea unless they have a copyright, trademark or patent to protect themselves and their creation, or I will steal it! It makes them think if they talk about their idea, it's free territory.

In most cases, it's something I am not interested in anyway, but you never know, and it scares them enough to make them think. Ideas have been stolen since the beginning of time, and someone has capitalized on them, so don't you be one of the victims! I must add though, that doesn't stop the person who came up with the idea from taking legal action to prove it was his or her idea! It's tough to prove, but it is possible. If you have an idea and it's worth keeping, keep it to yourself, and during those times when you can't keep it to yourself,

PROTECT YOURSELF!

Protect yourself with a confidentiality/non-disclosure agreement, which protects your information or inventions that are revealed during a meeting, discussion, negotiation or proposal.

**LAWS ARE ALWAYS CHANGING,
SO PLEASE SEEK LEGAL COUNSEL.**

Copyrights, Trademarks, and Patents

Now the rest of the story. After an unsuccessful attempt to license the product SLIM-PATCH to other firms, I decided to market the product myself. Never reaching the potential I had hope for, I later assigned the trademark registration of the name SLIM-PATCH over to a medical research company who was interested in marketing their own version of the product for the cost of my research and development. My point in this chapter is that you must protect yourself and your product by the legal means provided you through the Patent, Trademark and Copyright Offices or a lawyer specialized in the field. If you think you might have to spend a lot of cash to protect your invention, a legal consultation with a patent lawyer might just save you some cash, like it did me when I consulted a lawyer and was told a patent could not be applied for. The trademark protected my product with it's name: SLIM-PATCH. If I had never applied for that trademark on my product, anyone could have used my idea with the same name.

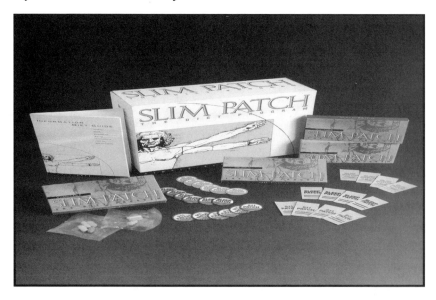

Chapter Three
Copyrights

Copyright is a form of protection provided by the laws of the United States (title 17, U.S. Code) to the authors of "original works of authorship," including literary, dramatic, musical, artistic, and certain other intellectual works. Section 106 of the 1976 Copyright Act generally gives the owner of copyright the exclusive right to do and to authorize others to do the following:

- **To reproduce** the work in copies or phonorecords;

- To prepare **derivative works** based upon the work;

- **To distribute copies or phonorecords** of the work to the public by sale or other transfer of ownership, or by rental, lease, or lending;

- **To perform the work publicly**, in the case of literary, musical, dramatic, and choreographic works, pantomimes, and motion pictures and other audiovisual works;

- **To display the copyrighted work publicly**, in the case of literary, musical, dramatic, and choreographic works, pantomimes, and pictorial, graphic, or sculptural works, including the individual images of a motion picture or other audiovisual work;

- In the case of **sound recordings**, **to perform the work publicly** by means of a **digital audio transmission**.

Copyrights

You can register your copyright with the U.S. Copyright Office, which is a federal agency, under the Library of Congress. It requires a small application fee, and it is located in Washington, D.C., where you can write or call for your forms. (Or go online). *You are not required to file for a copyright under law*, but if you don't, make sure your phrasing for the copyright is correct. If you are registering your copyright there are several different forms for specific areas of copyrights to choose from. So, be sure to be clear about your subject matter so you receive the right forms to fill out and file. They will send everything you need for your copyright protection. There are many do's and don'ts when it comes to copyrighting. There are so many that complete books have been written on the subject. I do not intend to enter the legalities of copyrighting. It is my intention only to write about the basics.

Copyright protection subsists from the time the work is created in fixed form. The copyright in the work of authorship *immediately* becomes the property of the author who created the work. Only the author or those deriving their rights through the author can rightfully claim copyright. In the case of works made for hire, **the employer** and **not** the employee is considered to be the author. *Minors may claim copyright*, but state laws may regulate the business dealings involving copyrights owned by minors. For information on relevant state laws, involving a minor, consult a registered patent attorney. **A work that is created (fixed in tangible form for the first time) on or after January 1, 1978, is automatically protected from the moment of its creation and is ordinarily given a term enduring for the author's life plus an additional 70 years after the author's death**. *In the case of "a joint work prepared by two or more authors who did not work for hire," the term lasts for 70 years after the last surviving author's death*. For works made for hire, the duration of copyright will be 95 years from publication or 120 years from creation, whichever is shorter.

Copyrights

To copyright your creation and notify others that you are the creator under U.S. copyright protection laws, (there is no such thing as an "international copyright" that will automatically protect an author's writings throughout the entire world) you have only a few items to comply with. Here's how simple it is. The notice for visually perceptible copies should contain all the following three elements:

First: add the copyright symbol: ©

Second: add the year: 2015

Third: follow it by your name: Victor N. Vic-Vincent

Example: © 2015 Victor N. Vic-Vincent

(You can use the word "Copyright," or the abbreviation, "Copr."; rather than the symbol). My material is copyrighted by this same example in the front of this book, so I had better be right! In many instances, you may have seen or have written statements yourself that you have believed legal to copyright your material such as "This work is protected by copyright," "All rights reserved," (by itself) or just plain "Copyrighted." Not so! These terms are <u>not</u> copyright correct and do not maintain your copyright ownership. Even worse, if these works are made public and these terms are used, the creator may forfeit his or her copyright rights. For sound recordings, the steps are basically the same; only a "P" is used instead of a "C," and the same rules apply. "This song may not be recorded," or "Protected" are not acceptable and will be treated as such. The letter "P" was added, so the general public could recognize the difference in literary works and sounds in material objects. (See Chapter Four on Music Publishing for more info).

Copyrights

Our interest in copyrights, as in patents and trademarks, is the legal ownership of our work to keep others from infringing on our product. With a **registered** copyright, we are entitled to all of the protection available under the 1976 Act. This keeps others from using our creation without our permission and allows us to profit from it ourselves. We can also profit from our copyright by licensing it to others or transferring ownership to others; if our copyright is used without our consent, we have the right to seek an injunction for infringement and sue for damages of a monetary value. Copyrights are inexpensive and easy to do yourself. So protect and register your work with the Copyright Office. (See the end of this chapter for online fee schedules and application forms). If your copyright is not registered, you may not have protection in a lawsuit. This copyright law permits us to profit from our creation without having to worry about others copying and profiting from it.

Works by the U. S. Government are not eligible for U.S. copyright protection. For works published on and after March 1, 1989, the previous notice requirement for works consisting primarily of one or more U.S. Government works has been eliminated. *However, use of a notice on such a work will defeat a claim of innocent infringement* as previously described provided the notice also includes a statement that identifies either those portions of the work in which copyright is claimed or those portions that constitute U.S. Government material.

Example: © 2015 Victor N. Vic-Vincent. Copyright claimed in Chapters 1-16, exclusive of U.S. Government works and maps.

U.S. citizens are given the right to use Government works without copyright infringement (luckily because I copy their material all the time) (LOL), but copies of works published before March 1, 1989, that consist primarily of one or more works of the U.S. Government **should** have a notice and a identifying statement like the one above.

Copyrights

When I created "The Decision Maker!," an executive desk plaque, I had copyrighted these gimmick names because this product used many small phrases inscribed on a name plate to design the desk plaque. The executive desk plaque had different inscriptions on it with a removable toy  gun that worked and looked just like a real gun. The names varied, and you had a choice of which to buy such as:

"Go Ahead Make My Day!"
"The Headache Reliever!"
"The Decision Maker!"
"The Stress Reliever!"
"The Pain Killer!"
or "Top Gun!"

But what I found out later was titles, words and short phrases are not copyrightable. They could possibly be trademarked but the cost outweighed the risk. So I believed a simple phrase would have caused no legality issues. (Personal opinion: nothing is ever set in stone, so get legal advice on any question you might have about your product's name). What's great about creating these type of gimmick products is that they can be done at a much lower cost when a trademark or patent is not required. You can go to **www.inventorsUSA.com** with any questions you might want to ask on copyrights. The information is free, but for free legal advice go to any search engine and type in **free legal advice** and you will be bombarded with free legal information websites. My online experience was great and every question I asked was responded to by an attorney. (Sometimes paralegals answer your questions).

Copyrights

Although a copyright registration is not required, the Copyright Act establishes a mandatory deposit requirement for works published in the United States. In general, the owner of copyright or the owner of the exclusive right of publication in the work has a legal obligation to deposit in the Copyright Office, within 3 months of publication in the United States, two copies (or in the case of sound recordings, two phonorecords) for use of the Library of Congress. Failure to make the deposit can result in fines and other penalties but does not affect copyright protection. If you elect to file a copyright claim, you may send in your copies with the correct application form and fee to the Copyright Office. They will make the deposit for you. **Note: A Library of Congress Control Number** is different from a copyright registration number. The Cataloging in Publication (CIP) Division of the Library of Congress is responsible for assigning LC Control Numbers and is operationally separate from the Copyright Office.

A book may be registered in or deposited with the Copyright Office but not necessarily catalogued and added to the Library's collections. (For Information about obtaining a Library of Congress Control Number, see Chapter Five on Book Publishing). Applications and fees received without appropriate copies, phonorecords, or identifying material will not be processed and ordinarily will be returned. **Unpublished deposits** without applications or fees ordinarily will be returned, also. In most cases, **published deposits** received without applications and fees can be immediately transferred to the collections of the Library of Congress. After the deposit is received and transferred to another service unit of the Library for its collections or other disposition, it is no longer available to the Copyright Office. If you wish to register the work, you must deposit additional copies or phonorecords with your application and fee. So, just do it right the first time. Don't do anything as important as this in haste. Complete all the required items, then file.

Copyrights

It's important to take the correct steps and protect yourself with someone familiar with these laws so you can relax and feel confident that you are protected and get on with the subject at hand: making money from your creation.

Here is a list of the different forms used for registering copyrights. Choose the form that fits your needs and order it through the Copyright Office or go online and print them out.

LIST OF APPLICATION FORMS

For Original Registration

Form PA. Form SE. Form SR. Form TX. Form VA. Form G/DN. Short Form/SE and Form SE/Group. Short Forms TX, PA and VA.
Form GATT and Form GATT/GRP.

For Renewal Registration

Form RE. Form RE Addendum.

For Corrections and Amplifications

Form CA.

For a Group of Contributions to Periodicals

Form GR/CP.

Copyrights

Form PA: *Use Form PA for registration of published or unpublished works of the performing arts.* This class includes works prepared for the purpose of being "performed" directly before an audience or indirectly "by means of any device or process." Works of the performing arts include (1) musical works, including any accompanying words; (2) dramatic works, including any accompanying music; (3) pantomimes and choreographic works; and (4) motion pictures and other audiovisual works.

Short Form PA: Short version of application for original registration.

Form SE: *Use a separate Form SE for registration of each individual issue of a serial, Class SE. A serial is defined as a work issued or intended to be issued in successive parts bearing numerical or chronological designations and intended to be continued indefinitely.* This class includes a variety of works: periodicals; newspapers; annuals; the journals, proceedings, trans-actions, et cetera, of societies. Do not use form SE to register an individual contribution to a serial. Request Form TX.

Short Form/SE: Specialized SE forms for use when certain requirements are met. These are designed to make registering large groups of work under the SE qualifications easier. All the following conditions must be met in order to use this form. If any one of the conditions does not apply, you must use Form SE. Incorrect use of this form will result in a delay in your registration.

1. The claim must be in a collective work.
2. The work must be essentially an all-new collective work or issue.
3. The author must be a citizen or domiciliary of the United States.
4. The work must be a work for hire.

Short Form/SE: (continued).
5. The author(s) and claimant(s) must be the same person(s) or organization(s).
6. The work must be first published in the United States.

Form SE/GROUP: All the following conditions must be used in order to use this form. If any one of the conditions does not apply, you must register the issues separately using Form SE or Short Form SE.

1. You must have given a complimentary subscription for two copies of the serial to the Library of Congress, confirmed by letter to: Library of Congress
   Group Periodicals Registration
   Washington, D.C. 20540-4161
   Subscription copies must be mailed separately to the same address.
2. The claim must be in the collective works.
3. The works must be essentially all new collective works or issues.
4. Each issue must be a work made for hire.
5. The author(s) and claimant(s) must be the same person(s) or organization(s) for all issues.
6. Each issue must have been created no more than 1 year prior to publication.
7. All issues in the group must have been published within the same calendar year.

For copyright purposes, serials are defined as works issued or intended to be issued in successive parts bearing numerical or chronological designations and intended to be continued indefinitely. The classification "serial" includes periodicals, newspapers, magazines, bulletins, newsletters, annuals, journals, proceedings of societies, and other similar works.

Copyrights

Form SR: *Use Form SR for registration of published or unpublished sound recordings, that is, for registration of the particular sounds or recorded performance.* Sound recordings are defined in the law as "works that result from the fixation of a series of musical, spoken, or other sounds, but not including the sounds accompanying a motion picture or other audiovisual work." Common examples include recordings of music, drama, or lectures. Copyright in a sound recording protects the particular series of sounds "fixed" (embodied in a recording) against unauthorized reproduction and revision, unauthorized distribution of phonorecords containing those sounds, and certain unauthorized performances by means of a digital audio transmission.

Form SR must also be used if you wish to make one registration for both the sound recording and the underlying work (the musical composition, dramatic, or literary work). You may make a single registration only if the copyright claimant is the same for both the sound recording and the underlying work. In this case, the authorship statement in Space 2 of this Form SR should specify that the claim covers both works.

Form TX: *Use Form TX for the registration of published or unpublished nondramatic literary works,* excluding periodicals or serial issues. This class includes a wide variety of works: fiction, nonfiction, poetry, textbooks, reference works, directories, catalogs, advertising copy, compilations of information, and computer programs. For periodicals and serials, use form SE.

Short Form TX: Short version of application for original registration.

Form VA: *Use Form VA for copyright registration of published or unpublished works of the visual arts.*

Copyrights

Form VA: (continued). This category consists of "pictorial, graphic, or sculptural works," including two-dimensional and three-dimensional works of fine, graphic, and applied art, photographs, prints and art reproductions, maps, globes, charts, technical drawings, diagrams, and models.

Short Form VA: Short version of application for original registration.

Form G/DN: A specialized form to register a complete month's issues of a daily newspaper when certain conditions are met.

Form GATT: Specialized form to register a claim in a work in which U. S. copyright was restored under the 1994 Uruguay Round Agreements Acts (URAA).

Form GATT/GRP: *Use form GATT/GRP to register copyright claims in a group of related works in which U. S. copyright was restored under the 1994 Uruguay Round Agreements Acts (URAA).*

Form RE: (Renewal Registration Form). *Use Form RE for claims to renew copyright in works copyrighted under the law in effect through December 31, 1977 (1909 Copyright Act) and registered during the initial 28-year copyright term.* For works copyrighted before January 1, 1978, the copyright law provides a first term of copyright protection lasting 28 years followed by a second term of protection known as the renewal term. However, these works were required to be renewed within strict time limits to obtain a second term of copyright protection. If copyright was originally secured before January 1, 1964, and was <u>not</u> renewed at the proper time, copyright protection expired permanently at the end of the 28th year of the first term and could <u>not</u> be renewed.

Copyrights

Form RE: (continued). Public Law 102-307, enacted on June 26, 1992, amended the copyright law with respect to works copyrighted between January 1, 1964, and December 31, 1977, to secure *automatically* the second term of copyright and to make renewal registration optional. The renewal term automatically vests in the party entitled to claim renewal on December thirty first of the 28th year of the first term. **Public Law 105-298, enacted on October 27, 1998**, extended the renewal term an additional 20 years for all works still under copyright, whether in their first term or renewal term at the time the law became effective. The 1992 and 1998 amendments do not retroactively restore copyright to U.S. works that are in the public domain. For information concerning the restoration of copyright in certain foreign works under the 1994 Uruguay Round Agreements Act, request the proper Circular.

Form RE: Addendum: (Renewal Registration Form Supplement). Accompanies Form RE for claims to renew copyright in works copyrighted under the 1909 Copyright Act but never registered during their initial 28-year copyright term. There is an additional fee for filing this Addendum.

Form CA: *Use Form CA when an earlier registration has been completed in the Copyright Office and some of the facts given in that registration are incorrect or incomplete and you want to place the correct or complete facts on record.* Form CA is used for supplementary registration to correct or amplify information given in the Copyright Office record of an earlier registration. As a rule, only one basic copyright registration can be made for the same work. To take care of cases where information in the basic registration turns out to be incorrect or incomplete, section 408(d) of the copyright law provides for "the filing of an application for supplementary registration, to correct an error in a copyright registration or to amplify the information given in a registration."

Copyrights

Form GR/CP: An adjunct application to be used for registration of a group of contributions to periodicals in addition to an application Form TX, PA, or VA. Form GR/CP is the appropriate adjunct application form to use when you are submitting a basic application on Form TX, Form PA, or Form VA, for a group of works that qualify for a single registration under section 408 (c)(2) of the copyright statute. It is not acceptable unless submitted together with Form TX, PA, or VA. All the works must have the same author.

To sum up Copyrights, here is a list of categories that are Copyrightable works:

1) Literary works.
2) Musical works, including any accompanying words.
3) Dramatic works, including any accompanying music.
4) Pantomimes and choreographic works.
5) Pictorial, graphic, and sculptural works.
6) Motion pictures and other audiovisual works.
7) Sound recordings.
8) Architectural works.

A copyright registration is effective on the date the Copyright Office receives all the required elements in acceptable form, regardless of how long it then takes to process the application and mail the certificate of registration. The time the Copyright Office requires to process an application varies, depending on the amount of material the Office is receiving. If you apply for copyright registration, you will not receive an acknowledgment that your application has been received (the Office receives more than 600,000 applications annually), but you can expect a letter or a telephone call from a staff member if further information is needed or a certificate of registration indicating that the work has been registered, or if the application <u>cannot</u> be accepted, a letter explaining why.

Copyrights

In general, copyright registration is a legal formality intended to make a public record of the basic facts of a particular copyright. However, registration is not a condition of copyright protection. Even though registration is not a requirement for protection, the copyright law provides several inducements or advantages to encourage copyright owners to make registration. Among these advantages are the following:

- *Registration establishes a public record of the copyright claim.

- Before an infringement suit may be filed in court, registration is necessary to establish U.S. origin.

- If made before or within 5 years of publication, registration will establish prima facie evidence in court of the validity of the copyright and of the facts stated in the certificate.

- If registration is made within 3 months after publication of the work or prior to an infringement of the work, statutory damages and attorney's fees will be available to the copyright owner in court actions. Otherwise, only an award of actual damages and profits is available to the copyright owner.

- Registration allows the owner of the copyright to record the registration with the U. S. Customs Service for protection against the importation of infringing copies. For additional information, request Publication "How to Protect Your Intellectual Property Right," from U.S. Customs Service or visit their website at **www.customs.gov** for online publications.

*To register a work for copyright you need only to file a properly completed application form. Enclose a nonrefundable application fee and two non-returnable deposits of the work being published.

Copyright Assistance

All these previous categories should be viewed quite broadly, and any question as how to file your particular creation can be answered by the Copyright Office free of charge.

If you know which application forms or circulars you want, request them from the Forms and Publications Hotline at:
(202) 707-9100
24 hours a day. Leave a recorded message.

If you are unsure which form or circular to order, call:
The Public Information Office number at (202) 707-3000.
TTY: (202) 707-6737
Information specialists are on duty from
8:30 a.m. to 5:00 p.m. Monday through Friday,
eastern time, except federal holidays.

Information by regular mail: Write to:
Library of Congress
Copyright Office
Publications Section, LM-455
101 Independence Avenue, S.E.
Washington, D.C. 20559-6000

Information via the Internet
Circulars, announcements, regulations, other related materials, and all copyright application forms are available from the Copyright Office Website at:
www.copyright.gov

The Public Information Office: Open to the public is located at:
Library of Congress, James Madison Memorial Building,
Room 401, 101 Independence Avenue, S.E., Washington, D.C.,
near the Capitol South Metro Stop.

General Information
www.inventorsUSA.com

COPY OF SONGWRITER DEMO SONGS SENT ON CD TO THE U.S. COPYRIGHT OFFICE FOR REGISTRATION. TWO COPIES OF THE DEMO ALBUM AND A COMPLETED REGISTRATION FORM **SR**, ALONG WITH PAYMENT WAS ALL THAT WAS NEEDED TO PROTECT MY SONG RIGHTS.

Chapter Four
Music Publishing

The copyright forms you need to fill out for your compositions are simple and they will protect your songs, words, music, words and music, arrangements, and recordings. So, what's the problem? Why do so many artists elect to have others do it for them? Do they get confused with all the different subclasses they see under copyrights? Maybe, and because of that, they hire an attorney. Big mistake! All they had to do was take the time to read the information. So, artists, veterans and amateurs, I'm here to set the <u>record</u> straight. You can do it yourself! The U.S. Copyright Office could not have made it any simpler.

 Not only is it inexpensive but the online website gives you easy step by step instructions you can follow to safeguard even your unpublished works. Go to the U.S. Copyright Office official website **www.copyright.gov** and print out Form PA: (Performing Arts) and the instructions. Form PA will be the form you fill out for musical works, including any accompanying words. For instance, your music composition (arrangement), the words to the song or both. You can file for them separate or together. Maybe you only wrote the words right now but didn't write the music arrangement yet. You can file just the words. Or, vice versa and file the other part later. If you wrote both the words and the music arrangements, file them on one form, form PA: (Performing Arts).

Music Publishing

If you have more than one song, say you are producing an album, just add them on a continuation sheet application form called CON. This makes it easy if you have written all the lyrics and music arrangements to your whole compilation but haven't recorded it yet. You can go ahead and file all your songs on one copyright application form for the one registration fee! Next, after you filed your PA copyright, your next step is to find a recording studio to produce your album. When it is complete, recorded to a "phonorecord," and you have the product in your hand, you will need to file Form SR (Sound Recording) if you are the only claimant; that is, if you are the same author for words, music arrangement and recording, file the finished product in a audio format, CD, MP3, et cetera) and make a single registration for all, with form SR. Send in your registration fee, along with your application (typed or written in black ink) and 1 copy of your work if it is unpublished, and two copies if it is published.

That's all there is to protecting your music. Now you will need to protect your music cover art-work (jacket covers for any media format); if you don't have any artwork, find a graphic artist, who can fulfill your image needs and produce your cover jackets. Here is an example of how important it is to make sure that you not only protect your music but you protect your complete "works" by registering it with the U.S. Copyright Office under the proper class and using the proper forms. In 1973, *Jefferson Airplane* released the album "Thirty Seconds Over Winterland." The album cover artwork consisted of a squadron of two-slice rounded toasters with clocks and white wings flying across the sky. In the late 1980s, a company called Berkeley Systems also liked the album cover artwork and used it in one of their screensaver software programs called "After Dark." Airplane registered the sound recording in the Copyright Office on Form N, which is specifically designed for registration of copyright in published sound recordings.

Music Publishing

They submitted with their application the record and the record jacket with artwork clearly visible. So, Airplane filed suit in June of 1994 claiming Berkeley infringed on their copyright. Berkeley's defense was the copyright registration that Airplane filed under Class N only extended to published sound recordings. Berkeley Systems argued and won that Class N (Before the new copyright law of 1976 went into effect, the application forms were designated by certain letters. Hence the Class N which was for sound recordings, is now SR and Class K was for artwork is now VA) registration was only for musical recordings and not for the artwork submitted. Airplane should have submitted a separate registration under Class K for the cover art. This Class K covers pictorial illustrations, cover prints and labels and prints used for articles of merchandise. The courts ruling agreed the album cover artwork satisfied all the copyright requirements for protection, but to win an infringement law suit, the law states that a registration must be made.

Airplane wanted to collect damages back to the time Berkeley introduced the "After Dark" software but the court ruled no infringement occurred. So, when filing for copyright protection keep this story in mind and make sure you file the proper forms. Check, double check, and triple check, and if unsure, call the Copyright Office. File your copyrights with a check or bank money order and two copies of your, "CD, audio format, et cetera." If your copyright claim is for original music, use the "c" in a circle notice: ©. If your copyright claim is for the production and engineering of a sound recording, use the "p" in a circle notice: ℗. You never know where your entrepreneurial skills will lead you. They have led me in many different directions, even music. Here is my personal story on how I learned about copyrights that pertain to music. A good friend of mine who owned a famous night club needed help promoting his business. One afternoon I came in early to work on some marketing issues and I ended up covering for a bartender who called in sick.

Music Publishing

While working behind the bar that afternoon, I kept hearing a wonderful voice (which I thought was on the radio) coming from the other side of the club. But as time went by, the singing would stop, then start again. It finally got the best of me. So, I went to change the radio station and to my surprise, the singing wasn't coming from the radio. It was coming from a gentleman playing his guitar and singing all alone in the dark. I struck up a conversation with him, and we became friends. The more I found out about his life, the more I wanted to help him. He was a famous rhythm and blues singer in the late 1960's early 70's, with several top ten hits and gold albums. Then he went blind, became a recluse and lived in a small shack that had no heat or air-conditioning with three other semi-homeless people. They stole from him. They ate his food. His situation was awful, and that needed to change.

So, I decided to hire a band. Now he could perform in the club and earn an income. In the meantime while he's packing the club with patrons, making the owner happy and making me look like a whiz kid, I made some inquiries into the music business and consulted with a few contacts in L. A. and before you knew it, we were on tour and he was famous again. For the next two years we traveled back and forth from Florida to California, giving concerts and making friends with many other famous singers and bands. His life changed and so did mine. Bobby Purify, singer of the songs, "I'm Your Puppet!", "Shake A Tailfeather!", (Both heard in the movies "Meet Your Parents" and "The Blues Brothers"), You Can't Keep A Good Man Down!", et cetera, was also a Grammy Nominee. We made television appearances, talked with disc jockeys on the radio, and when we weren't on tour, performed in night clubs throughout the country. When it came time for him to go on to bigger projects, I probably made music industry history. I sold my management contract for one dollar. They had a purpose. This group was going to produce a movie about his life and record a new album.

Music Publishing

I always believed what was ever right for Bobby was the right thing to do. He had been taken advantage of enough. I wasn't in it for the money. I was his friend first. So, I did what friends do. I let him go on and further his career, and I went on to further mine. Subsequently, while marketing yourself, always keep on a lookout for other opportunities that can open up different and exciting careers like what happened to me in this story above. While I was working for another client I happened onto an even bigger client.

And while marketing him, I marketed myself. I began writing songs for an album I would later produce. I didn't know a thing about the music business, I learned from those who did, then I protected and produced my music. I wrote and produced songs in different genres, like the country song, "Buck! Buck! Buck!", the rock song, "911, Code Red", the high energy song "X-tasy," and the swing song, "Hurricane Katy!" The words to the songs and the music arrangements were all copyrighted using Form PA. The sound recordings (music) would later be copyrighted using Form SR.

Music Publishing

I then created a publishing firm, so if I ever sold one of my songs, I would collect 100% and you should too. Example: If you are the author of a song and assigned the rights to a publisher, a contract is drawn up and the publisher will take a percentage of sales. (Usually 50%). The publisher then has to make a deal with your manuscript to music retailers, furthering your percentage drop. Create your own publishing firm and market your own work. In reality, once you have written your song, you are the song's publisher. Being a self publisher means you must solicit your music to record companies, recording artists, and producers, yourself. It means making and duplicating CD's, MP3's, DVD's, whatever the new technology is at the time, and mailing them out to whomever can benefit you. It means researching trade magazines, tip sheets and making long distance phone calls. This takes a considerable amount of time and money on your part.

But it's worth it, if your song becomes a hit on the music charts. Because instead of making 50% or less on your song, you are now making 100% of the publishing and writer's royalties. Your success will be determined on how determined you are. You must keep abreast of what's going on and where its going on. And get your songs to the right person. Ok, you have recorded your songs, you have obtained your copyrights, and protected your artwork. Now to be an official publishing company you must register your company name with one of the U.S. performing rights organizations (PRO) of your choice. There are three: ASCAP, BMI, SESAC. Once you have chosen a PRO and registered, they will search their records and officially clear your company name. Then when monies for your songs are due you from others using it on television broadcasts, nightclubs, radio, satellite radio, et cetera, one of these companies you have chosen will pay you your royalties. The primary function of the performing rights societies is to collect and distribute the royalties to the proper party.

Music Publishing

After you have registered your publishing company name, it would better serve you to sign on with the same performing rights organization as a songwriter as you did a publisher. If you have already copyrighted your songs, you will need to transfer them over to your publishing company using the proper forms with the copyright office. Then go back to the PRO you are using and fill out the percentage of the writer's and publisher's percentage on the clearance forms and where to send the royalty payments. Now that you have taken care of the music side of the publishing company, it's time to take care of the business side. Once your publishing name has been filed and cleared with a PRO, you will need to go to city hall and obtain a business license under this name. Then go to a bank and open a business account using your new company name. Now your in the music publishing business! That's all there is to it, and you did it yourself! Now here comes the advice, the advice I learned from many hours in the office and on the road experience.

The publishing company you just created was out of greed. The greed we all have, to keep all we make. Why should we give away 50% of our creative song writing and hard work to someone else? I know I said the same thing. Well here's the rest of the story! 50% of something is better than 100% of nothing. Publishing companies were formed for a reason: they have the contacts. Successful publishers set up meetings with recording artists and record labels. Their primary job is to generate income from the performance royalties and sales of your songs. This is how they make their money. I have mailed many a CD to people in the "BIZ," but you can bet I never got one of my songs heard until I used a publisher with inside contacts. I am not trying to dissuade you; I really want you to try on your own, but if you do not succeed, you still have an outlet and that is to use a reputable music publishing company. If you continue to concentrate on losing the 50% rather than using your energy to gain 50%, you will be fighting a losing battle.

Music Publishing

If your song has what it takes to secure a contract with a well-known recording artist, you will earn more than that 100% you never made on your own, which amounted to zero. If you intend to send your manuscript to other publishers for review, never send the original, make a copy and send that. Music publishing is one of the most important legal matters in a singer's, musician's, or band's career. The words and music composition to songs are very important to musicians and singers. For most this is their livelihood. So, treat it like a business. After the copyrights, the publishers, and the UPC codes for retail sale, you now need someone to track your music, if it is ever played in the media such as, Radio, Television, et cetera. You want to be paid your royalties. That's where your performing rights organization comes in. They will track your media play time and send you your royalties. The music business is a billion dollar industry. You are its creator. The songwriter. The music maker. Without you there would be no market. So get your share.

Produce your product, send out press kits, design websites, produce shows, advertise. Arrange a list of people you will need to move your career ahead of the many others trying to get there before you.

- Marketing People: To promote the band and sell your products.
- A Manager: To manage schedule of all parties involved, finances and scoring recording or publishing contracts.
- Booking Agent: To book your night club acts or tours.
- Entertainment Lawyer: To negotiate contracts.
- Publicist: To promote your career.

Along with all this, you will still be your own greatest sales person. You will still have to sell yourself. So in the meantime, while others are working on your career, don't you stop! Look for different venues to play at like Casinos, Coffee Houses; check new approaches to selling your music, like video game licensing. This is one of the fastest growing fields in the entertainment industry.

Music Publishing

Keep marketing yourself. If you <u>do</u> make it or <u>don't</u> make it as a superstar, you can still help others in their quest to stardom, just by the knowledge you obtained along the way; who knows, maybe that knowledge will turn into a career like it did Michael, creator of an online website for musicians, singers, bands, et cetera. "I use to be a couch potato who watched others succeed. I had a MILLION excuses for not going after what I CLAIMED to be able to achieve. It was much easier to talk a good game than it was to actually do it. Are you stuck in that rut? But, in 1992 I got hit by that bolt of lightening that got me off my butt. I worked harder than ever before, yet it didn't feel as hard as when I worked for other people. I was committed. I was determined. I was ENERGIZED! I loved what I was doing, so it was fun! Sure, there were plenty of times when I was at wit's end and ready to give up, but I didn't.

That's when I became part of the 2% who end up winning, instead of remaining part of the 98% who spend their lives talking about success, but never achieving it. Now I own a successful company whose clients span the globe. I earn my living by helping people achieve their own potential. I love my life. I love my "job." Can you look at yourself in the mirror and say that? I want you to be able to. I want everybody I know to experience the intense satisfaction that comes with creating your own success. And I am not just talking about music here. There might be something you're better at than music, something you'd love to do even more! You just need to set goals that are realistic. And take the first step. Then take another, and then another. Don't chicken out when you hit a road block or meet with rejection. That's what the 98% do, but not the 2% who are the world's wealthiest and most successful people. You can be a winner. I know because I've done it. I'm, Michael Laskow creator and CEO of **www.taxi.com**." Like Michael said, maybe there's something your better at than music, like writing a book. If so, the next chapter will show you how to self publish.

Music Publishing Assistance

For those serious about the music business, but have no formal training, one of the best colleges to attend is "FULL SAIL." For a real world education, they have one of the most excellent music and entertainment business programs available in the United States. FULL SAIL even has a degree program in Show Production and Touring which covers everything from life on the road, to live event production in as little as 13 months. Then there's the Entertainment Business where you can get a Bachelor of Science Degree in 9 months. You get training in marketing, advertising, accounting and finance. This training is enough to give you a lead in the entertainment field or prepares you for creating your own industry media business. They have full scale stage setups just like if you were on tour. If you get the chance, stop in and check this school out when you are in Orlando, Florida visiting Disney World. It's located at 3300 University Blvd. in Winter Park. If you're a band, they frequently need music performances to participate in student projects, and you can learn while there. Call for info: 1-407-551-1088.

Website: **www.fullsail.com**

There's another great place to visit: Mark Dreyer Productions in Nashville, Tennessee. I recorded a country song with a R&B recording artist. I liked the music but thought it needed a country flair. So, I contacted Mark, discussed the song and the music production, and he then gave me a reasonable rate and recorded it in country. His company will also help you find the people you need if they can't provide the service you are looking for, with their free referral assistance. It is also one of the best music websites for production I have seen for musicians. Check it out. They provide a direct camera linkup into their studio from their website. You can view nationally famous artists at work on your songs or others. So, if your looking for that Nashville sound for your lyrics, music or both call Mark Dreyer at 1-615-826-4141.

Website: **www.nashvilleconnection.com**

Music Publishing Assistance

- **PERFORMING RIGHTS ORGANIZATIONS**

Collects royalties on behalf of songwriters and composers.

- **ASCAP**

(American Society of Composers, Authors and Publishers).
One Lincoln Plaza
New York, NY 10023
Phone for members 1-800-952-7227
Website: **www.ascap.com**

- **BMI**

(Broadcast Music, Inc.)
320 West 57th Street
New York, NY 10019-3790
1-212-586-2000
Website: **www.bmi.com**

- **SESAC**

(Society of European Stage Authors & Composers).
152 West 57th ST
57th Floor
New York, NY 10019
1-212-586-3450
Website: **www.sesac.com**

- The Harry Fox Agency, Inc.

Represents music publishers for mechanical, digital and other electronic licensing needs. They collect and distribute royalties and issue licenses on behalf of their affiliated publishers. They are not a performing rights organization.
711 3rd Avenue, 8th Floor
New York, NY 10017
1-212-370-5330
Website: **www.harryfox.com**

BOOK SIGNING TOUR

Chapter Five
Book Publishing

I added this chapter on self publishing because it involves copyrights. When words are put to paper, Inventors become Writers, and creative Writers become Authors, and Authors need protection under the copyright law. My explanation for writing on the subject of publishing was not because of my expertise in this field, but it was because of my experience in the field. Maybe, what knowledge I gained can help you. I wrote and published this book myself. Why? Because I am not that wealthy that I can pay someone else to do my writing, like a lot of famous people do. For example, you see many books written on well known sports personalities, TV and movie stars; do you think these people write their own books?

No way, some big executive pays these celebrities a lot of money for his or her life story so that the big executive's publishing company can have its many writers, editors and printers, produce thousands and thousands of books about these illustrious people, sometimes in less time than it takes us to find a good word processing program for our computer. These celebrities don't have to lift a finger. They mostly talk into voice recorders. Well, we're not that lucky. We have to write, edit and publish our own books. At least for now, until our books make the best seller list, and we become a celebrity! Right!... Right!... But that comes later; for now you must stop fantasizing and come back to reality, a reality that means you must do it on your own and as cheaply as possible.

Book Publishing

There are many incentives for publishing and promoting your own book; here are a few. If a publishing company has one thousand customers, that's one thousand different books, how could they promote one thousand books? They can't; they would lose money. It would cost the publisher more than that Rolls Royce you see him or her driving, and he or she isn't about to give that up, not for your book that has about a one in a million chance of reaching the top ten best seller list! These subsidy publishers produce ads that are very attractive to the novice writer that may headline, "Authors wanted..." or "Manuscripts needed..." Beware of these ads because as with any product or idea, there are companies around that will take advantage of you and profit from you. (Honest literary companies do not need to advertise for authors and manuscripts). But I was hoping when I started this process of producing my book that the one field that would be honest would be the publishing field. No such luck. There are just as many sharks in the publishing industry as there are in the invention, idea industry.

Many of these publishing companies have fast talking sales people with beautiful brochures. They advertise that their company will publish and promote your book at cost. Why? Just like they tell you in the invention, idea industry, they will tell you in the publishing industry just what you want to hear! "Your book is the best thing I have ever read. It's sure to be a best seller!" Well, if you are as easily swayed by flattery as we all are, then you just got scammed! How? They will talk you into paying legal, marketing and setup costs associated with producing your book. The contract may be for ten thousand books, but they will only bind a couple of hundred books on the first run, and you will never know the difference because you will be given only a small number of copies to promote and sell your book. You will not be given anymore unless you pay for them. The book covers and binding can be expensive, so the rest of your copies will be printed on demand.

Book Publishing

They don't care whether your book sells or not, they just made a pretty hefty sum from the money you sent to cover publishing and marketing costs, but they don't need to market your book to make money, you do! And they won't print another batch until you sell what's already printed, so they have no risk! Oh yeah! Don't forget the contract you signed, not only did you forfeit your copyrights, but for any sales that you made, you were bound by contractual law to pay them a large percentage of those sales. Here's what happened to Samantha Lynn, author of the young adult book <u>The Mythical Sword of Devalon</u>. "I was seeking out publishers to publish my book when I came across a publishing company that I thought would be the best for me and my book. This seemingly legitimate publishing company agreed to produce, promote and market 10,000 books. I paid them over $3,000 and signed a contract that would give them 40% of the first 2,500 books sold and 15% thereafter.

Their contract asked for full control over the copyright. After a short negotiation I remained in control of my copyright and signed the contract. To abbreviate this story I received a small amount of my books for resale and got no marketing or publicity assistance from this publishing company. After many months of heated phone calls, I decided to promote the book myself. Then two years later they went out of business, leaving me to start all over again." Samanthas' story ends on a good note; she found a hardworking agent and is now promoting her third book. "It's hard enough trying to be a successful writer without being taken advantage of." She then adds, "Look out for the publisher in sheep's clothing. If you are the least bit lucky, the publishing company will show your book in one of their brochures. But this brochure won't be to promote sales of your book, it will be used to help promote sales to other un-suspecting writers for more of their publishing company prof-its." (Read more on companies that manipulate unsuspecting writers in Chapter Fifteen on Scams).

Book Publishing

Most likely this defunct publishing company Samantha Lynn used just reopened under a different name because several of these vanity publishers have been in trouble with the Federal Trade Commission. They try to stay just ahead of any legal action that may be brought against them, so they shut down just long enough to change names. Now don't be discouraged by the truth, because if you thought I was going to tell you that you didn't need any money and you didn't have to do anything but collect royalties, then you bought the wrong book. You want good honest and truthful information, and that's what I'm going to give you. Some day it may be the case that you can collect royalties from your book, but let's get real; we're nobody's that want to be somebody's, and to be somebody, we have to make a name for ourselves. Well, enough of what I don't recommend. Now lets go on to what I do recommend.

The first step will be to write your book. Again an idea for a book is nothing, and you will be paid what that's worth, NOTHING! Make your goals simple. Write one chapter at a time. Get your hands on a computer. Either buy one, borrow one or better yet go to your local public college or university and use one. Not just the students or faculty have access to the computers, it's the public. Why? Because you funded these colleges and universities with the taxes you paid, and the bond money the state gave these colleges and universities for these computers came from taxpayers. So these learning centers cannot deny you accessibility. The students will even show you how to use them. Then all you will need is some form of media memory to burn (copy) and save your work too. This will save you a lot of disappointment in case of a computer failure. (Get in the habit of saving your work as you write). Make sure your writing program has a spell checker. This is very helpful for correcting spelling errors. But do not forget to edit the writings yourself because these programs cannot find errors for correct spellings such as "their," when it's suppose to be, "there."

Book Publishing

Or, if you were writing a story on *baking* and you accidentally wrote *biking,* the spelling correction program would miss it and you most likely would too and your readers would be confused. That's why editing is so important. So, edit and re-edit, again and again, looking for errors. When your through writing each day, spell check your story. Give your book fancy headings and chapters with different letter fonts, styles and sizes. Font is the letter type like these letters which are called Times New Roman or these letters which are called Franklin Gothic Book or **even these which are called Courier New in Bold.** Styles are *Italic* and **bold.** Size like in this book is 12 point, or this 8 point, or even larger

sizes such as this 20 point in Arial. If

you are unsure what style headings and size to use for your book, just look through other books for ideas.

Make sure your printer is at least 360 dpi, that's three hundred and sixty *dots per inch.* The higher the number, say 720 dpi, the better the resolution for printing. My first book printing was with a 360 dpi printer, and it was just fine. Your book will require certain general and important information and this information is always found on the first two or three pages in the book. The first is your title page where you will have the name of your book and your editors name. The second is your copyright page where you will put in your ISBN#, CIP# and other assorted data you may not have received yet, and the third is your table of contents; leave all these pages blank for now. You can come back and fill in these pages when you have that data. This is important because if you print the whole book without leaving these pages open then you will have to reprint your whole book again because your page numbers will be off by two or three. (Unless you have automatic page numbering). This is also why you must create your front and back book cover in a different folder. (So it does not count these pages in your book).

Book Publishing

This way you won't have to keep changing page numbers that often. O.K. now your books final copy is printed, so put it aside for now because you will need to proceed to the smaller part of your book that's going to give you the biggest headache. We will start with a small pain, editing, and work our way up until we get a migraine looking for a printing company, that's when we will know we are just about ready for publishing, when our head is ready to explode. After you have finished writing your book, find an outside editor to edit your book. Because no matter how many times you edit it and how many times you edited it right, someone else will find a mistake or two. Now your thinking, this is going to cost me a lot of cash, experienced copy editors are very expensive. Well it won't. Go to your local university or college again and speak with someone in the literary department about having a student who will soon be graduating with a degree in English Literature to do the editing. Usually a student will be happy to get his or her career started by editing your manuscript.

Just mention his or her name as copy editor in the front of your book. But please be willing to pay them something for their time, remember they're saving you hundreds of dollars. Now your book is written and edited. Print it out on high quality paper so the printer can make good reproductions from your copies. (Or burn a copy to a disc in the printers format if they request one). Your book will require an ISBN **Bar code** if sold to the retail market and with today's high-tech scanning for prices, you will need to get an **ISBN** (International Standard Book Number). This number is the number used by retail stores and book stores to identify your book. You can call, write or go online: International Standard Book Numbering Agency, 1180 Avenue of Americas, New York City, NY 10036. Tell them you are requesting an ISBN. The company is R.R. Bowker and they are a large agency with many departments, so you must be specific when you write or call them for what you need.

Book Publishing

If you are only printing your book for personal use or private sales, you will not need this number; but if you plan on publishing your book for retail stores, then it's a must. You can then have this number printed up on bar code labels that you stick on yourself or have a bar code negative made up for the publisher to print on the back page of your book for scanning. (Example: The bar code on the back cover of this book). Do not print in the barcode space, leave it blank. The Printer will do this. Next we move on to the inside layout, to the *Copyright Page*. This is the page after your *Title Page* and it's the most important part of your book. This is where you will print your copyright notice which we already discussed in the section under copyrights. Your ISBN will be listed here also along with the name and address of the publisher, (which is you) and a Library of Congress Catalog Card Number. The Library of Congress gives out pre-assigned card numbers for your book.

You can get this Cataloging Number by calling or writing the CIP (Cataloging in Publication) Office, WA, D.C. 20540. Request a "Library of Congress Catalog Card Number" application form or apply online. Then when you receive this number you can type it in the front of your book along with the ISBN before your book is published. Also add, printed in the "United States of America." This will help you avoid complications in the future if the need ever arises that you want to export your book. Now we need to work on the book cover. If you need artwork or graphics that require professionals, then use the professionals. If you don't, then use a computer again to create your graphics artwork and large letter type. When choosing colors, black and white is the cheapest but colors attract attention. Use whatever colors it takes to get the buyer's attention. Just remember, the more colors you choose for your cover, the more your book will cost to print. This cover was published in this design & color not because it was cheaper, but because I wanted to get your attention amongst all the other book covers.

Book Publishing

I don't want to complicate the process of producing your first book, so this pretty much covers the basic process of writing and producing your own book. If you need more specific information, there are many books out there that will go into a greater detail on publishing. But my best advice is to just pick up other books, look at their covers, look at their back pages, look on the inside pages, and make decisions from what you see. After your book is completed from front to back, we now have to find a printer. Look close to home for local printers; if they cannot print your book, they usually can refer you to some one who can. If there are no printers in your area, don't fret; many books have been printed without the author ever meeting the publisher, The Inventor's Cookbook Your Recipe For Success!, my first book, is an example.

I never met my printer; I looked in the "Thomas Register," found a couple of book printing companies close to my home, and called these companies for quotes. After receiving several bids and talking with several representatives always on their 1-800 line, I picked one and sent them a copy of my book. From there it was just a matter of time before I received my first shipment. It was a proud day for me when they arrived at my front door; it was a great feeling of triumph. Don't let yourself be stopped by negative thoughts; if Mark Twain or Hemmingway didn't let themselves be stopped by all the hardships they had to endure, then you shouldn't either. Heck, they didn't even have a word processor! If you still feel you can't afford to print your book after you received your quotes, then there is one alternative. You can have your book duplicated on a copy machine then punched and spiral bound. Don't laugh! I actually produced The Inventor's Cookbook by spiral binding before I ever had it published in perfect bound form for the most common reason. I didn't have enough money for one-thousand perfect bound books, and I was afraid if I borrowed that much money to produce my book, I may not sell enough to recoup my losses.

Book Publishing

So, I had the pages of fifty books double-sided copied on a copy machine. Then I produced a color cover and back page on my computer. I printed it out on sturdy 110lb paper with my computer color printer, then borrowed a punch and binding machine at a local office supply store. (Check around because many office supply stores have a section in the store where they work duplicating and binding customers media presentations). You can get your book copied there and buy the plastic spiral binding combs; then use their binding machine for free. My first book was published this way and cost me about five dollars to produce one. Not bad for self publishing. So I produced about fifty books, test marketed them, and did so well, I decided to take the risk. Honestly I didn't know how my book would be perceived in spiral form, I was worried it looked too amateurish, but what I found out was the public was focused on the information not the packaging. Also look into online publishing.

Your e-book is printed or downloaded to the buyer on demand directly to their computer. It is a fast and economical way of producing your book. Here's a few more good tips on how to save money. If you do mail order and ship your books through the U.S. Post Office, ask for the book rate because its much cheaper than the first-class rate. Create your own publishing company and take the tax advantages for having your own business. Try to set up an autograph signing in some of the minor and major book stores. There is no cost to you, and you get free publicity. Contact your local newspaper for a book review and keep promoting; the only way you can become successful with your book is if the public knows where to buy it. Remember you can test market your book yourself by publishing it yourself. (The difference between a publishing company and a printing company is a printing company is only interested in producing your book, not marketing and selling it like a publisher). So use a printer for binding or spiral bind your book yourself, and promote and market it yourself to reap all the profits yourself!

Book Publishing

Here is a story of co-incidence I feel compelled to write. When I was starting out as a writer, I did a lot of research and read a lot of books. One book stood out: The Self-Publishing Manual, first printed in 1979, by Dan Poynter. I followed the basics and used his knowledge of publishing and wrote my first book, The Inventor's Cookbook Your Recipe For Success! This year while researching updates for self-publishing on the internet, I came across a site that offered good free advice to writers. I contacted them for some research information, and lo and behold, the website was created by none other than Dan Poynter. With all the thousands of publisher websites, it was truly a remarkable coincidence. Again he offered great free advice on his site, and I feel a sense of gratitude to share that with you. His website is located at **www.parapub.com**, and I believe you will find his information valuable in your hopes and dreams of becoming a published author.

Imagine being a published author. Picture people coming up to you at a meeting with a copy of your book and requesting an autograph. Visualize passing a bookstore and seeing your book in the window. Consider being interviewed for an article. Imagine the fame that comes with being published. People think if you wrote a book, you know something. And you probably do. When you think about it, you are writing your book from the very best research plus your personal experience and knowledge. Writing a book is a creative act; selling it is a business. Some people can do both while others are more creative than businesslike. You have to ask if you want to be a publisher. Do you have an office, the time to conduct the business and a place to store the books? If you do, go to Dan's site **www.parapub.com** and research his information, and use his years of experience to create your own novel or self-help book. (I am not associated with Dan's site or Para Publishing in anyway and this is not a paid advertisement). His knowledge helped me. Maybe it can help you.

Book Publishing Assistance

I have found two websites that have made publishing your book so easy that you have no excuse not to. The first, Booksurge, **www.booksurge.com** now an amazon.com company, helps self-publishers become authors. They publish, edit, refine, market, distribute through e-books and have your paperback available for viewing at industry trade shows. I personally have checked out the pricing and have found all the costs reasonable, especially for the first time author. They can even provide ISBN's for your manuscript. For those who are already authors it provides another avenue to promote and get your book into the mainstream market of retail and online buyers. They also have royalty agreements between you and them. The royalty rate is as follows: (Examples subject to change).

- 25% on sales of retail books.
- 10% royalties on all bookstore orders.
- 70% on sales of the electronic files.

(As of this date, royalties on hardcover books are less). Royalty rates allowed through these programs are higher than normal rates paid in the book industry. Which is commonly 10%.

The second is **www.cafepress.com**, I like this website because it deals with the entrepreneur not just in books but other products as well. Plus they give you a free store available to sell up to 70 different products when they are produced by CafePress.com. They have a special section on books to help you design and create your layouts and will offer support. They are not a full-fledged book publisher, but after viewing and studying the information, I like being a store owner where I can sell my books and my creations. Being a part owner of **www.springbreakinc.com** it was perfect for us. We opened our store with only the very basics in cost, and it runs itself almost virtually without any assistance from us. We receive royalty/commission checks from our product sales, deposited directly into our account. It is money we would otherwise never be making.

Book Publishing Assistance

- File for your book copyright using form TX with the U.S. Copyright Office. **www.copyright.gov** *Note*: Your are unable to trademark a book title, because you may have several titles with the same name, ex: "THE TITANIC" but the stories may be on completely separate subjects. One ships, the other planes.
- If you sell a book and an audiocassette which is deemed a multimedia kit file form SR.
- File for your Library of Congress Control Number (LCCN) with the Cataloging in Publication Program (CIP). **www.loc.gov**

Note: There is no charge for CIP processing, but participating publishers (that's you as a self publisher) are obligated to send one complimentary copy of your book for which the CIP data was provided (your Library of Congress Control Number) immediately upon publication. If you fail to do so, you may be suspended from the program.　　　　Library of Congress
Cataloging in Publication Division
101 Independence Avenue, S.E.
Washington, D.C. 20540-4320
www.loc.gov

- File for your ISBN (International Standard Book Number). **www.isbn.org** Click on the arrow in the submit box and bring up ISBN Application. This site is for first time publishers. The Library of Congress does not administer or distribute International Standard Book Numbers. Contact R.R. Bowker:
630 Central Avenue
New Providence, NJ 07974
Tel: 877-310-7333　Fax: 908-665-2895
www.isbn.org/standards/home/isbn/us/

- Order your barcode negative. When you receive your ISBN number, click on Bar Code Suppliers on the Bowker website.
www.isbn.org
 - Find a printer and have your book printed!

Chapter Six
Trademarks

A trademark is different from a patent or a copyright. A patent protects an invention. A copyright protects an original artistic or literary work. A trademark is a word, phrase, symbol or design, or a combination of words, phrases, symbols or designs, that identifies and distinguishes the source of the goods of one party from those of others. Trademarks are the way manufacturers identify their products. A trademark can also identify the ownership of merchandise to which it is applied for the exclusive use of the owner or owners under the Trademark Federal Registration laws. Unlike patents or copyrights, trademark rights can last indefinitely if the owner continues to use the mark to identify the product, services, or corporation and files the declaration and renewals timely.

You have the right to register a trademark with the Patent and Trademark Office (PTO) if you intend to use a mark or if you are using a mark. For you do-it-your-selvers, file the Trademark/Service Mark Application online. (See the last pages of this chapter for online filing and information). The application must be filed in the name of the owner of the mark, (that's you), partnership, or corporation. You may submit the application, or you may have an attorney represent you. The term for a federal trademark registration is ten years with ten year renewal terms, but to keep the trademark alive, you must file a Declaration of Use of a Mark under Section 8, specimen, and fee on a date that falls on or between the fifth (5th) and sixth (6th) anniversaries of the registration. You are responsible for filing this Declaration. You will not receive a notice.

Trademarks

FAILURE TO FILE A SECTION 8 DECLARATION WILL RE-SULT IN CANCELLATION OF THE REGISTRATION. If your trademark is approved, do <u>not</u> miss filing this important declaration, or your registration will be canceled. One of the most significant steps will be coming up with a brand name for your product one that everyone can associate with your creation. Like COKE, this name has the distinction of serving mankind with a name that is associated with all cola drinks as CHIQUITA is associated with all bananas. Whatever name you choose to trademark, make it *sizzle*! Think hard when coming up with your trademark name. You want it to stand out; you want it to reach out and grab you. You want a name that people will see and remember. So, if they like what they see and can remember the name, they can tell their friends and their friends will tell their friends about your product, and, when they go shopping, they can ask for it by name and buy it.

Good trademark names are easy to remember, easy to say, and easy to recognize. They should not contain words in general use like automobile, airplane or hamburger et cetera. Try to use a name that you believe no one has ever used, something very creative. If you are going to have a trademark name search done by a lawyer, you don't want the name to show up during the search because every time your name shows up, you have to create another name and pay for another search. Even if you are going to do the name search yourself, you will still have the time and work associated with researching again, so try to be very creative in naming your product. Also, if you are planning to market this product overseas, your trademark name may be a very good American saying, but in a different language, it could be disastrous. Check your foreign dictionary for the correct spelling and definition. Then double-check using a translator. Your U.S. Trademark, Patent, or Copyrights are not protected in other countries, so file for them in the country you are doing business in.

Trademarks

This name search is what you will do or have done before you file for a trademark approval. So be sure the name you picked is not already trademarked. If it is, then you could be infringing on someone else's product. This is the reason for trademarks to begin with: so no one else uses your name to associate a product similar to yours. There is an exception; some names can already be in use and you could still use them like "McDonalds." Yes, you could use this name, but the key is, you better not be making hamburgers. You could, however, be making doors, and your company name could be "McDonalds Doors," if you file under the classification for doors and get approved. I created hand-painted men's and women's neck ties, and I was looking for a distinctive name, a name that said excitement, and I came up with **"*FIZZIES*."** This name had been used, a long time ago, to promote a seltzer flavored drink that fizzed when you dropped the tablets in a glass of water. I liked the name and used it for my ties, and this name was approved.

That's because it was in no way associated with the beverage and I filed under class 025 (clothing). This is not a concrete rule however; if any firm thinks that the name you picked will be detrimental to their business, they could file a law suit, even if your trademark has been approved. So talk to your lawyer, but try not to create a name that will cause you any legal problems. That way, you can devote all your time to making your product a success without having someone looking over your shoulder, waiting to put a stop to you, if you infringe on their mark. Let's talk about games and gimmicks for a minute. If you plan to create a board game, you can relax; in most cases you do <u>not</u> have to file for a patent. I created the board game **"*Bankruptcy*!"** by just *trademarking* the name and *copyrighting* the game's rules and instructions. This protected the name of the product and the way it is played, but it did not protect the product or the product's design. For this a design patent may have been useful for the board layout, but not really necessary.

Trademarks

If your game or gimmick is unique in any way, then seek a patent for protection; however, it would be very hard for someone or some company to recreate a game without following the same set of rules, and this is what I based my decision on. If you want to protect the game's design or if your game or gimmick has a distinctive component, seek a patent. As for the trademark, first create a name, have a name search completed by a registered trademark and patent attorney or agent, or do the search yourself, and file for trademark protection. The cost for a trademark search by an attorney is fairly inexpensive. You can decide if you want to spend the time searching yourself or pay an attorney to handle all the details. I found the cost about the same if you consider the time and cost spent traveling to and from a research center. Although, you may find the cost worth the experience or you may be close to a patent and trademark library. If so, by all means, go and do the search yourself! It will be a great learning experience. You can also go online to the patent and trademark website (USPTO) and search records free of charge if you have access to a computer.

Trademark Assistance

Benefits of Federal Trademark Registration.

1. Constructive notice nationwide of the trademark owner's claim.
2. Evidence of ownership of the trademark.
3. Jurisdiction of federal courts may be invoked.
4. Registration can be used as a basis for obtaining registration in foreign countries.
5. Registration may be filed with U.S. Customs Service to prevent importation of infringing foreign goods.

Filing Trademark Applications Online:

Go to **www.uspto.gov**. On the homepage of the Patent and Trademark Office under Trademarks, click on **File**. This brings you to the **Trademark Electronic Application System** for filing online. Under **Forms** select **Apply for a New mark**. This will bring you to the **Trademark/Servicemark Application**, **Principal Register** (You). Click on this. Now you're on the **Certification Mark Form**, **Principal Register** (You). Use the form wizard for the trademark Application. It's automatic unless you select the standard form. (Suggest you stay with the form wizard). The PTO office has tried to make this form as simple as possible to use online, and if you are uncertain of any section, you can click on any subject (in blue) on that line and get the information you need. You are now on your way to obtaining a Trademark. It's that easy! **Helpful Hint**: At the bottom of all the form pages there are help buttons to answer questions you might have. Just click on Help or Trademarks FAQ. Very informative information. Anytime you get confused just click on Home, also at the bottom of the page, and this will bring you back to start. (Home Page). *At the time of writing this book I am filing for a trademark name that was previously approved then abandoned (DEAD) under the classification code 025: Goods and Services: clothing. Keep informed of my progress on my website at:* **www.inventorsUSA.com**. *It should be interesting and prove helpful if you ever file for a trademark of an abandoned name.*

Trademark Assistance

On the homepage of USPTO, go to bottom of page and click on USPTO Fee Schedule for updated costs for filing Trademarks. To locate a **Patent and Trademark Library** near you call 1-800-786-9199 or visit the USPTO website at **Patent and Trademark Depository Library** Program (PTDLP) page. They offer access to trademark reference materials and search tools. If your fortunate enough to be close to the main search facility located in Alexandria, VA, Go! Trained staff are available to assist public users. Here is the address:

Public Search Facility - Madison East,
1st Floor
600 Dulany St.
Alexandria, VA 22313

They offer classes, onsite search assistance and state of the art computer workstations. To file a paper trademark application form you must call the Trademark Assistance Center at
1-800-786-9199 or 1-703-308-9000
Request one, fill it out and mail it in with your payment.
However, the paper forms are not
processed as quickly as those submitted electronically.

Internet Direct
Trademark Application Online:
Trademark Electronic Application System (TEAS)
http://www.uspto.gov/teas/index.html

Basic Trademark Information
http://www.uspto.gov/main/trademarks.htm
Provides a wide variety of information about trademarks and offers electronic filing of trademark applications and other trademark documents. *Good place to start.*

Trademark Assistance

Trademark Assistance Center
E-mail: TrademarkAssistanceCenter@uspto.gov
Phone: 1-571-272-9401

USPTO website for filing trademarks: **http://www.uspto.gov**
Questions on Trademarks E-mail: **TEAS@uspto.gov**
Trademark Technical Glitches E-mail: **teas@uspto.gov**
Status of Trademark Application website: **http://tarr.uspto.gov**

Trademark search using TESS
(Trademark Electronic Search System) Website.

**http://tess2.uspto.gov/bin/gate.exe?
f=login&p_lang=English&p_d=trmk**

For all other questions concerning USPTO programs
& services call the USPTO Contact Center:
1-800-786-9199.

For **Patent/Trademark Attorneys and Agents** authorized to represent inventors before the U.S. Patent and Trademark Office. (Also known as the Attorneys Roster and Patent Attorneys Roster File). General Information Services will provide a list of names of attorneys and agents within a mileage radius of a particular city, zip code, or state if you do not have web access call 1-800-786-9199 or 1-703-308-4357. If you have web access go to USPTO homepage. Go to very bottom of page and click on Trademark Attorney. Go to very bottom of that page and click on search. Type in Trademark Attorney Roster. Scroll down till you find OED—Registered Attorney/Agent search. Click on it. You will see Search Notes. Where it says Search For, type in your zip code. A list of Attorneys in your area will come up. It's that simple. (OED stands for OFFICE OF ENROLLMENT AND DISCIPLINE).

Chapter Seven
Patents

A patent for an invention is the grant of a property right to the inventor, issued by the Patent and Trademark Office. The term of a new patent (utility) is 20 years from the date on which the application for the patent was filed in the United States (all applicants will receive a dated and serial number filing receipt from the PTO) or, in special cases, from the date an earlier related application was filed, subject to the payment of maintenance fees. Maintenance fees are required for **all utility patents** filed on and after December 12, 1980, and are due every 3 ½, 7 ½ and 11 ½ years from the date the patent is granted and can be paid without a surcharge during the "window period" which is the six month period <u>preceding</u> each due date, e.g., 3 to 3 years and 6 months.

Failure to pay the current maintenance fees on time may result in expiration of the patent. A six month grace period is provided when the maintenance fee may be paid with a surcharge. The grace period is the six month period immediately following the due date. The Patent and Trademark Office does not mail notices to patent owners that maintenance fees are due, so keep track of your maintenance fee due dates. This is really important, so set a reminder. Don't lose your patent rights. U.S. patent grants are effective only within the U.S., U.S. territories, and U.S. possessions. The right conferred by the patent grant is, in the language of the statute and of the grant itself, "the right to exclude others from making, using, offering for sale, or selling" the invention in the United States or "importing" the invention into the United States.

Patents

What is granted is <u>not</u> the right to make, use, offer for sale, sell or import, but the right to exclude others from making, using, offering for sale, selling or importing the invention. If you plan to do business outside the United States, be sure to protect your invention in that country under their patent laws. Make sure your invention is safeguarded before you send any samples to a foreign country because that country can take your creation, reproduce it, and sell it, and you would not receive even a penny! As a U.S. citizen, if you decide you want to protect your invention in other countries, you must file an application in the patent office of each country within the time frame of the patent laws. (There is no such thing as an international patent). Say you wanted to do business in Hong Kong, but were afraid of someone stealing your idea and profiting from it without your consent. In such a case, it may be worth the expense; otherwise, this may prove to be a very costly task. Consult with an attorney on international laws, and then make your decision.

To research foreign patent treaty regulations go to the USPTO website. Type in the search box "international patents." If you are a foreign citizen, you may also obtain a U.S. patent if you comply with all the provisions under the patent law just like a U.S. citizen, but the U.S. patent protects your invention only in this country. The patent application must be filed in the English language or be accompanied by a verified translation in the English language. A patent <u>cannot</u> be obtained upon a mere idea or suggestion. In order for an invention to be patentable it must be new as defined in the patent law, which provides that an invention <u>cannot</u> be patented if: "(a) the invention was known or used by others in this country, or patented or described in a printed publication in this or a foreign country, before the invention thereof by the applicant for patent," or "(b) the invention was patented or described in a printed publication in this or a foreign country or in public use or on sale in this country more than 1 year prior to the application for patent in the United States."

Patents

If the invention has been described in a printed publication anywhere in the world, or if it has been in public use or on sale in this country before the date that the applicant made his/her invention, a patent cannot be obtained. According to the law, only the inventor may apply for a patent (with certain exceptions). If a person who is not the inventor should apply for a patent, the patent, if it were obtained, would be invalid. The person applying in such a case who falsely states that he/she is the inventor would also be subject to criminal penalties. If two or more persons make an invention jointly, they apply for a patent as joint inventors. If one of the persons is only a financial contributor, he/she is not a joint inventor and cannot be joined in the application as an inventor. However, it is possible to correct an innocent mistake in erroneously omitting an inventor or in erroneously naming a person as an inventor.

This chapter will sum up almost everything you will need to know on submitting different patent applications, but in no way can I give you specifics on any one subject. Patent applications are complicated. If they weren't, we wouldn't need patent attorneys or thousands of pages of data on how to file them. You will have to make the decision to use a legal representative or to do it yourself after you have studied the downloaded information you received from the USPTO website. I do suggest that you contact a patent attorney before you file your application, even if you plan on filing it yourself because it's very important to find out if your invention is even patentable. The patent attorney is intelligent enough to make that decision because he specializes in this area. You could save yourself a lot of grief if your attorney advises you that your invention is unpatentable and, if it is patentable, give you a clear conscience that you are on your way to realizing your dream! While getting your funds together to file for a patent, file a disclosure document with the United States Patent and Trademark Office. It is a very small fee, and it will offer you some degree of comfort.

Patents

This disclosure is accepted as evidence of the conception of your invention although in <u>no</u> way does it protect you like a patent; but, at least it offers some small reassurance of protection for up to two years. There is no special form to fill out for the **Disclosure Document Program**. All you have to do is draw and describe your invention on standard size paper not to exceed 8 1/2 by 11 inches in size. Number and date each page. Write a declaration stating you are the inventor and request that the material be reviewed for processing under the Disclosure Document Program and ***duplicate it***. Accompany these papers with a stamped, self-addressed envelope with the required small fee. The duplicate paper will be stamped with an identifying number and returned for your records. Photographs are also accepted. For more information on this program contact the USPTO at: **1-703-308-4357** and read the last section in this chapter on the Disclosure Documents.

If you have not created your product yet because you don't know how to get your idea manufactured, the first step is to find an engineer. Have the engineer sign a confidentiality agreement; then tell him or her about your concept because if you are unsure  about the exact way you want it produced, an engineer can give you guidance. Then locate a draftsperson so he/she can make detail drawings from your description or the description the engineer provided for you. You need a product to get a patent, and this draftsperson can draw up the blueprints that a manufacturer will understand. Take these blueprints to a manufacturer and have a prototype manufactured. Remember an idea is not an invention and is not patentable until it is (created), manufactured. A utility patent, in general, can be quite expensive to the average working person. It may take up to two years or longer, and there are no guarantees of approval. If your patent is not approved, normally it can be overcome with a qualified patent attorney or if you have the skills to re-file.

Patents

Nine out of ten patents are rejected; if this happens just correct the problem or problems and re-file. Expect it to be rejected, then you won't be disappointed. You can save yourself a lot of money by doing it yourself if your invention is not very complicated; but, unless you have a strong engineering and drafting background and are very literate, I suggest you pay the experts. If it's worth patenting, it's worth a patent attorney. Many people file patents themselves only to end up having an attorney to re-file for them, and it ends up costing them more. Do not be afraid to reveal all of your invention verbally or in documentation to your attorney or your trusted witnesses, for, if you leave anything out in your application for a patent, you could be doing yourself an injustice. If you created an invention and left out the most important part for fear of it being copied, then you just allowed that very same thing to happen to you because when you created your invention, the most important item was not patented and can now be used by others.

The documentation in your notebook will protect you, and, besides, patent attorneys are bound by very strict laws. Some creations may not even require a patent; they may only require a trademark or copyright, and a patent attorney can make that decision. It's important to find out because there are big differences in costs concerning which type of application you file! (Patent, Trademark or Copyright). Patent costs can go well into the thousands of dollars, not including the patent search done by an attorney, or you can do the search yourself at one of the several patent libraries. Like the trademark, it must be researched to make sure that you are not infringing on someone else's invention, creation, or design. Complicated patent applications can be very expensive, even if you do it yourself. So if you are like most of us and you live day to day with your finances and you believe you have created this million dollar idea, you are going to have to take a chance and try to find someone who can finance you and your patent application.

Patents

If you must seek out a qualified attorney for your patent application, make sure he or she is registered with the United States Patent and Trademark Office. There is a list you can obtain of those lawyers or agents who have been examined by this office and found to be qualified patent representatives. Only registered attorneys or agents can submit your application, and it is illegal for anyone to represent him or herself as a patent attorney or agent if he or she is not one. This is for your protection so you can be assured of getting the best application applied for as possible. You can also write or call for a list of qualified trademark and patent attorneys in your area. This roster is also available on the World Wide Web.

http://www.uspto.gov

Even though they must be qualified attorneys or agents listed with the United States Patent and Trademark Office, that does not mean they all charge the same. Ask several different practitioners for estimates and research them. Ask around, and as with anything else, don't just go by the price because sometimes, as the saying goes, "you get what you pay for!" The patent law is very important because without it, many people would not pursue their ideas, and the general public would not get the opportunity to use their creations, and new patents stimulate production of more inventions. O.K., now it's time to run down the steps you should take in obtaining a patent.

Patents

1. Think about your product. Make sure that you believe it's a worthwhile invention before you undertake the cost, time, and effort you will have to put forth to obtain a patent. Then call or write the Patent and Trademark Office for the application forms or go online.

2. Have someone trustworthy sign his or her name as a witness on a dated drawing and description of the invention from its conception. You may find this important later when you try to prove the date when you first conceived the idea. Even better, make and keep a dated documented record of the steps you take with receipts. Have a notary witness, sign, and stamp your records as you progress.

3. File a disclosure document or provisional application with the Patent and Trademark Office. This disclosure document will stay on file for two years to document the dates your invention was conceived. For better documented protection, file the provisional patent application which will protect your creation for up to one year before you file for non-provisional patent protection.

4. Have a patent search performed for the main reason of finding out if your creation has ever been invented before. (You do not want to file a patent application and undergo all the expense to find out later your invention has already been invented). Also, you can compare the other inventions found in this search to yours, and if it is not the exact same, you may be able to use some of this information to prepare your patent application.

5. Follow up the progress on your filed application. If you change anything during the time your application was filed, send in an Amendment Transmittal Letter obtained through the USPTO.

6. Because laws change, contact the United States Patent and Trademark Office just before you file your application to make sure you are using the correct forms and paying the correct filing fees.

Patents

Do it yourself! (Summary). For you hard-core entrepreneurs who want to file your patent application yourselves, it's time consuming, and you risk being denied a patent for minor things such as using the wrong terminology; but it can be done. Here's how. Call the USPTO for patent forms or go online. **Then purchase or borrow the following office supplies if you do not already own them: *Paper.*** *8 1/2 by 11. Flexible, strong, white, smooth, nonshiny and durable.* ***Pens.*** *Black indelible drawing pens. (India ink).* ***Notebook.*** To hold all your patent information and drawings. *A good* ***typewriter*** *and/or a* ***computer***. *Large strong* ***mailing envelopes***. (You can go online and get precise information from the USPTO website). You will be continually updating your creation, so you want to do all your scratch work in your notebook and date each one of your sketches. When it's all completed, do a final draft of your drawings. This drawing should be clear, clean, and concise because this is the one you will submit with your application.

This drawing or drawings will help the examiner who is reading your application understand its use. Every part of your drawing must be numbered and referred to in the written part of your patent application as required by patent law. Do this work yourself, and, if upon review, the examiner finds your drawings unacceptable, you may want to hire a professional draft person. If drawing by hand, use a good quality drawing pen and black indelible ink. Keep the drawings to a minimum, and make them as simple as possible. If drawings are from a computer they must be direct printouts. You may use color drawings or photos in certain circumstances if you file a petition with the USPTO requesting they be accepted. All papers in the specification including claims must be written by either a typewriter or mechanical printer in permanent dark ink on but one side. No hand lettering and/or initials are allowed except for signature requirements. In the do-it-yourself version of patenting, I suggest that you look for other inventions such as yours.

Patents

Find out what their patent numbers are (you can do this by going to any store that carries inventions such as yours and just by picking up the item, look on the packaging for the patent approval number) and have the USPTO research these applications and send you copies in the mail if you desire but the quickest and simplest way is to go online. Type the patent # in the search box and BAM, there's the patent, complete with drawings. You can download a hundred pages per minute if you have a cable modem for a minimal fee. Those inventors must have done something right because they were granted a patent, so it will be highly regarded information to use when applying for your patent. They also make a great guide when drawing up your application. If you do not find any inventions like yours and have searched online, and you are positive, (the important word here is P O S I T I V E) you are the only one with this invention, then you do not have to do a patent search.

The patent examiner does a search of your creation when he receives your patent application and filing fee, and if the examiners search does not reveal another invention like yours, you saved some money; if he does find one, you could lose your filing fees. So be sure your invention is truly one of a kind. If any doubt exists, have an attorney do a search. I am not recommending that letting the patent examiner do your search is your best avenue of approach, but, if you are positive, and again I say P O S I T I V E !, you can save the lawyer's fees associated with the search. The examiner will make sure it is truly one of a kind, and you will not be charged for the search; it's the patent examiner's job. If your invention does come back unapproved for any reason, this does not mean the end to your creation. You can review the unapproved patent, make changes, and file for an amendment. You can talk directly to your patent examiner who may be able to guide you in the right direction. You can make this call free of charge. By calling the toll free phone number at the United States Patent and Trademark Office.

Patents

You will need to prepare your application by following the guidelines put out to you by USPTO and the following pages. These pages will be boring but important information to follow when it comes to preparing the filing of your documents and drawings for a patent. *These regulations are set up by the United States Patent Office and are subject to change at any time.* If you have any trouble with wording or certain claims, the examiners can help you with the proper terminology. If you are close to the Patent and Trademark Office, you can benefit from their services by being able to arrange a meeting with the examiners; however, most of the correspondence is done in writing, e-mail or by phone. If you decide you want to undertake the risks of filing a patent yourself, go ahead. Do it yourself! If you need help, call the USPTO for answers to your questions. It's a government office; the consultants work for the taxpayers. If you file for a patent yourself, **claim a small entity status**. (Small entity is an independent inventor, a nonprofit organization, or a small business concern). You can save half the cost of the patent filing charges.

There are three types of patents:
Utility, Design, and Plant.

- **Utility** patents may be granted to anyone who invents or discovers any new and useful process, machine, article of manufacture, or compositions of matters, or any new useful improvement thereof,
- **Design** patents may be granted to anyone who invents a new, original, and ornamental design for an article of manufacture, and,
- **Plant** patents may be granted to anyone who invents or discovers and asexually reproduce any distinct and new variety of plants.

There are two types of utility and plant patent applications:
Provisional and Non-Provisional.

SPECIAL
DOOR

Requirements For Filing a
PROVISIONAL
Patent Application

A provisional application for patent is a U.S. national application for patent filed in the USPTO under 35 U.S.C.§111(b). It allows filing without a formal patent claim, oath or declaration, or any information disclosure (prior art) statement. It provides the means to establish an early effective filing date in a non-provisional patent application filed under 35 U.S.C.§111(a). It also allows the term "Patent Pending" to be applied. Since June 8, 1995, the USPTO has offered inventors the option of filing a provisional application for patent which was designed to provide a lower-cost first patent filing in the U.S. and to give U.S. applicants parity with foreign applicants under the GATT Uruguay Round Agreements. A provisional application for patent has a pendency lasting 12 months from the date the provisional application is filed. **The 12-month pendency period <u>cannot</u> be extended**.

Therefore, an applicant who files a provisional application must file a corresponding non-provisional application for patent (non-provisional application) during the 12-month pendency period of the provisional application in order to benefit from the earlier filing of the provisional application. In accordance with 35 U.S.C. §119 (e), the corresponding non-provisional application must contain or be amended to contain a specific reference to the provisional application. The provisional application must be made in the name(s) of all of the inventor(s). It can be filed up to one year following the date of first sale, offer for sale, public use, or publication of the invention. (These pre-filing disclosures, although protected in the United States, may preclude patenting in foreign countries).

A filing date will be accorded to a provisional application only when it contains the following:

- a written description of the invention, complying with all requirements of 35 U.S.C.§112¶ 1 and
- any drawings necessary to understand the invention, complying with 35 U.S.C. §113.

If either of these items are missing or incomplete, **no** filing date will be accorded to the provisional application.

To be complete, a provisional application must also include the filing fee as set forth in 37 CFR.1.16(k) and a cover sheet identifying:

- the application as a provisional application for patent;
- the name(s) of all inventors;
- inventor residence(s);
- title of the invention;
- name and registration number of attorney or agent and docket number (if applicable);
- correspondence address; and
- any US Government agency that has a property interest.

Advantages of applying for a provisional application:

- Establishes an official United States patent application filing date for the invention.
- Provides simplified filing with a lower initial investment with one full year to assess the invention's commercial potential before committing to the higher cost of filing and prosecuting a non-provisional application for patent.
- By filing a provisional application first, and then filing a corresponding non-provisional application that references the provisional application within the 12-month provisional application pendency period, a patent term endpoint may be extended by as much as 12 months.

- Permits one year's authorization to use **"Patent Pending"** notice in connection with the invention.

- Enables immediate commercial promotion of the invention with greater security against having the invention stolen.

This information is general in nature and is not meant to substitute for advice provided by a patent practitioner. Applicants unfamiliar with the requirements of U.S. patent law and procedures should consult an attorney or agent registered to practice before the USPTO.

By claiming small entity status and complying with all the provisional filing application paperwork, you can establish an internationally recognized U.S. filing date, and for a period of up to 12 months after filing, it can be converted into a Non-Provisional Application claiming the benefit of an earlier filing date. *"This allows the provisional patent application to be used as a filing date for your invention. This period can benefit the inventor by allowing time to seek licensing or funding to develop the inventor's invention."* (Quoted by Don Kelly; Director for The U.S. Patent and Trademark Office on the subject of patent applications). *"Another important benefit,"* Mr. Don Kelly added, *"is the 20 year term would be measured from the date of filing of the complete Non-provisional application, not the Provisional!"* **The patent examining group director, Don Kelly from the United States Patent and Trademark Office** (during the time of this interview) went on to say, *"Provisional patent applications are, in many ways, simpler and easier to file than the non-provisional patent applications, but you should understand that a provisional application does not give rise to the same substantive rights provided by non-provisional applications.*

This is because a provisional application is not examined and will not issue as a patent. Instead, provisional applications provide only a right of priority, that is, an established filing date. That's not to say this isn't a very important benefit. The filing date is recognized in major countries throughout the world. Another important point to note about provisional applications is that there will be no benefits of any kind if a non-provisional application is not filed within the 12-month period that follows the filing of the provisional application. Some filers assume that there is an automatic conversion from provisional to non-provisional that occurs within the Patent and Trademark Office. Not true! Positive steps must be taken and they must be taken within the noted time period. A provisional application does not require a declaration or claims, but meeting these filing requirements can't be taken lightly.

Invention disclosures presented in provisional applications must be just as thorough and clear as would be required in non-provisional applications. Since the purpose of the provisional application, as I've already noted, is to establish a recognized filing date for a subsequent non-provisional application to be filed within twelve months, heavy reliance will be placed on the completeness of the originally submitted invention disclosure. Claims defining the scope of applicant's invention filed in the subsequent nonprovisional application must find full and clear support in the original provisional application in order to gain full benefit of the early filing date." The Provisional patent application is a very inexpensive way for the inventor to protect his invention allowing him/her time to find an investor or manufacturer licensing agreement. In the meantime, after you have filed your provisional patent application, start working on all your non-provisional patent paperwork so you will be able to file this right away in case you find a financial backer or you sell the licensing rights to a manufacturer.

Patents
PROVISIONAL PATENT APPLICATION

Carry your non-disclosure agreement with you (even though your invention is now considered "Patent Pending" when you filed your provisional patent application), and make sure he or she signs it before you disclose any information about your invention. The more you protect yourself the better. If an investor files any patent application for you, make sure your name is on the patent as the inventor. Your investor or manufacturer is not the inventor and cannot be included on your application as an inventor!

For Forms, Publications, And Website Information For Filing Patents Refer To This Information Below.

A brochure on Provisional Application for Patent is available by calling the PTO General Information Services at 1-800-786-9199 or 1-703-308-4357 or by accessing PTO's Web site at:

http://www.uspto.gov/web/offices/pac/provapp.htm

Fees are subject to change annually. The current fee for a provisional application for patent can be found on the fee page of the USPTO website, or call the USPTO Contact Center Division (UCCD). Customer service representatives are available Monday through Friday (except Federal holidays) at 1-800-786-9199 to provide information on patents fees and answer any questions you might have.

The Inventors Assistance Center (IAC) provides patent information and services to the public. The IAC is staffed by former Supervisory Patent Examiners and experienced Primary Examiners who answer general questions concerning patent examining policy and procedure. Send e-mail to **independentinventor@uspto.gov**.

Patents

Provisional Patents Warnings And Cautions

- Independent inventors should fully understand that a provisional application will not mature into a granted patent without further submissions by the inventor. *Some invention promotion firms* misuse the provisional application process leaving the inventor with no patent.

- A provisional application automatically becomes abandoned when its pendency expires 12 months after the provisional application filing date by operation of law. Applicants must file a non-provisional application claiming benefit of the earlier provisional application filing date in the USPTO before the provisional application pendency period expires in order to preserve any benefit from the provisional application filing.

- Effective November 29, 2000, a claim under 35 U.S.C. 119(e) for the benefit of a prior provisional application must be filed during the pendency of the non-provisional application, and within four months of the non-provisional application filing date or within sixteen months of the provisional application filing date (whichever is later). See 37 CFR 1.78 as amended effective November 29, 2000.

- Provisional applications are not examined on their merits.

- It is recommended that the disclosure of the invention in the provisional application be as complete as possible. In order to obtain the benefit of the filing date of a provisional application the claimed subject matter in the later filed non-provisional application must have support in the provisional application.

- Provisional Applications for Patent may <u>not</u> be filed for design inventions.

Requirements For Filing a
NON-PROVISIONAL
Utility Patent Application

Each year the USPTO receives approximately 300,000 patent applications. Most of these are for non-provisional <u>utility</u> patents. A non-provisional utility patent application must be in the English language or be accompanied by a verified translation in the English language and a fee set forth in 37 CFR §1.17(i) {Non-English Specification Fee Code 139}.

All papers which are to become part of the permanent records of the USPTO must be typewritten or produced by a mechanical (or computer) printer. The text must be in permanent black ink or its equivalent on a single side of the paper, in portrait orientation on white paper that is **all of the same size**, flexible, strong, smooth, nonshiny, durable, and without holes.

The paper size must be either
- 21.6 cm. by 27.9 cm. (8 1/2 by 11 inches), or
- 21.0 cm. by 29.7 cm. (DIN size A4).

There must be a left margin of at least 2.5 cm. (one inch) and top, right and bottom margins of at least 2.0 cm. (3/4 inch). Drawing page requirements are on the same size paper but require different margins et cetera, (see Drawing Requirements). A nonprovisional utility patent application *must* include a specification, including a claim or claims, drawings, when necessary, an oath or declaration, and the prescribed filing fee.

A complete nonprovisional utility patent application *should* contain the elements listed below, arranged in the order shown.

1. Utility Patent Application Transmittal Form or Transmittal Letter.
2. Fee Transmittal Form and Appropriate Fee.
3. Application Data Sheet (see 37 CFR § 1.76).
4. Specification (with at least one claim).
5. Drawings (when necessary).
6. Oath or Declaration.
7. Nucleotide and/or Amino Acid Sequence Listing (when necessary).

All the above elements are described below in numerical order. These descriptions are brief. View the complete application requirements online or order the guide directly from the USPTO.

1). A UTILITY PATENT APPLICATION TRANSMITTAL FORM (Form PTO/SB/05) OR TRANSMITTAL LETTER A transmittal form or letter should be filed with every patent application to instruct the USPTO as to what actual types of papers are being filed (e.g., specification, claims, drawings, declaration, information disclosure statement). It identifies the name of the applicant, the type of application, the title of the invention, the contents of the application, and any accompanying enclosures. (Form PTO/SB/21 is to be used for all correspondence after initial filing).

2). FEE TRANSMITTAL FORM The Fee Transmittal Form (Form PTO/SB/17) may be used to calculate the prescribed filing fees and indicate the method of payment, by check or by credit card. The amount and type of filing fees are dependent upon the number and type of claims presented. Fees are subject to change and the applicant should consult the current *Fee Schedule* before filing. Check to see if you qualify for the small entity discount fee.

3). APPLICATION DATA SHEET The application data sheet is a sheet or sheets, that may be voluntarily submitted in either provisional or nonprovisional applications, which contains bibliographic data arranged in a format specified by the USPTO. Specific bibliographic data includes applicant information, correspondence information, application information, representative information, domestic priority information, foreign priority information and assignment information. (See 37 CFR § 1.76). The sheets must be produced according to a format provided by the USPTO, which is downloadable to applicant's computer. Supplemental application data sheets may be subsequently supplied prior to payment of issue fee to either correct or update information in a previously submitted application data sheet, or an oath or declaration under title 37 CFR § 1.63 or 1.67. Supplemental application data sheets should indicate the information that is being supplemented, and therefore need not and should not contain information previously supplied that has not changed.

4). SPECIFICATION The specification is a written description of the invention and of the manner and process of making and using the same. The specification must be in such full, clear, concise, and exact terms as to enable any person skilled in the art or science to which the invention pertains to make and use the same. The page numbers should be centrally located preferably below the text. The lines of the specification must be 1.5 or double spaced (lines of text not comprising the specification need not be one and a halve or double spaced). It is desirable to include an indentation at the beginning of each new paragraph, and for paragraphs to be numbered (0001 et cetera). **It is preferable to use all of the section headings described on next page** to represent the parts of the specification. Section headings should be in upper case without underlining or bold type. If the section contains no text, the phrase "Not Applicable" should follow the section heading.

a).   *TITLE OF INVENTION.* The title of the invention (or an introductory portion stating the name, citizenship, residence of each applicant, and the title of the invention) should appear as the heading on the first page of the specification. Although a title may have up to 500 characters, the title must be as short and specific as possible.

b).   *CROSS-REFERENCE TO RELATED APPLICA-TIONS.* Any nonprovisional utility patent application claiming the benefit of one or more prior filed copending nonprovisional applications (or international applications designating the United States of America) under 35 USC §§ 120, 121 or 365{c} must contain in the first sentence of the specification following the title, a reference to each such prior application, identifying it by the application number or international application number and international filing date, and indicating the relationship of the applications, or include the reference to the earlier application in an application data sheet. (See 37 CFR § 1.76). Cross-reference to other related patent applications may be made when appropriate.

c).   *STATEMENT REGARDING FEDERALLY SPON-SORED RESEARCH OR DEVELOPMENT.* The application should contain a statement as to rights to inventions made under federally sponsored research and development (if any).

d).   *REFERENCE TO SEQUENCE LISTING, A TABLE, OR A COMPUTER PROGRAM LISTING COMPACT DISC AP-PENDIX.* Any material submitted separately on a compact disc must be referenced in the specification. The only disclosure material accepted on compact disc are computer program listings, gene sequence listings and tables of information.

e). *BRIEF SUMMARY OF THE INVENTION.* This section should present the substance or general idea of the claimed invention in summarized form. The summary may point out the advantages of the invention of how it solves previously existing problems, preferably those problems identified in the "Background of the Invention." A statement of the object of the invention may also be included.

f). *BRIEF DESCRIPTION OF THE SEVERAL VIEWS OF THE DRAWING.* Where there are drawings, you must include a listing of all figures by number (e.g., Figure 1A) and with corresponding statements explaining what each figure depicts.

g). *DETAILED DESCRIPTION OF THE INVENTION.* In this section, the invention must be explained along with the process of making and using the invention in full, clear, concise, and exact terms. This section should distinguish the invention from other inventions and from what is old and describe completely the process, machine, manufacture, composition of matter, or improvement invented. In the case of an improvement, the description should be confined to the specific improvement and to the parts that necessarily cooperate with it or which are necessary to completely understand the invention. It is required that the description be sufficient so that any person of ordinary skill in the pertinent art, science, or area could make and use the invention without extensive experimentation. The best mode contemplated by you of carrying out your invention must be set forth in the description. This section has often, in the past, been titled "Description of the Preferred Embodiment."

h). *CLAIM or CLAIMS.* The claim or claims must particularly point out and distinctly claim the subject matter which you regard as the invention. The claims define the scope of the patent.

h).   *CLAIM or "CLAIMS. (Continued).* Whether a patent will be granted is determined, in large measure, by the choice of wording of the claims. A nonprovisional application for a utility patent must contain at least one claim. The claim or claims section must begin on a separate sheet. If there are several claims, they shall be numbered consecutively in Arabic numerals, with the least restrictive claim presented as claim number 1. The claims section must begin with a statement such as "What I claim as my invention is..." or "I (We) claim..." followed by the recitation of the particular matter which you regard as your invention. One or more claims may be presented in dependent form, referring back to and further limiting another claim or claims in the same application.

All dependent claims should be grouped together with the claim or claims to which they refer to the extent practicable. Any dependent claim which refers to more than one other claim ("a multiple dependent claim") shall refer to such other claims in the alternative only. Each claim should be a single sentence, and where a claim sets forth a number of elements or steps, each element or step of the claim should be separated by a line indentation. The fee required to be submitted with a nonprovisional utility patent application is, in part, determined by the number of claims, independent claims, and dependent claims.

i).   *ABSTRACT OF THE DISCLOSURE.* The purpose of the abstract is to enable the United States Patent and Trademark Office and the public to determine quickly the nature of the technical disclosures of your invention. The abstract points out what is new in the art to which your invention pertains. It should be in narrative form and generally limited to a single paragraph, and it must commence on a separate page.

i).   *ABSTRACT OF THE DISCLOSURE. (Continued).* An abstract should not be longer than 150 words.

5). DRAWINGS (When necessary). A patent application is required to contain drawings if drawings are necessary for the understanding of the subject matter sought to be patented. The drawings must show every feature of the invention as specified in the claims. Omission of drawings may cause an application to be considered incomplete. An application for a design patent must contain at least one drawing.

DRAWING REQUIREMENTS

Information on drawing requirements is based substantially on 37 CFR § 1.84. There are two acceptable categories for presenting drawings in **utility patent** applications: black ink (black and white) and color. Black and white drawings are normally required. India ink, or its equivalent that secures black solid lines, must be used for drawings. Drawings made by computer printer should be originals, not photocopies. On rare occasions, color drawings may be necessary as the only practical medium by which the subject matter sought to be patented in a utility patent application is disclosed. The USPTO will accept color drawings in utility patent applications and statutory invention registrations only after granting a petition explaining why the color drawings are necessary. Any such petition must include the following:

- The appropriate fee set forth in 37 CFR § 1.17(h).

- Three (3) sets of color drawings.

DRAWING REQUIREMENTS (Continued).

- The following language as the first paragraph in that portion of the specification relating to the BRIEF DESCRIPTION OF THE SEVERAL VIEWS OF THE DRAWING. If the language is not in the specification, an amendment to insert the language must accompany the petition.

"*The patent or application file contains at least one drawing executed in color. Copies of this patent or patent application publication with color drawing(s) will be provided by the Office upon request and payment of the necessary fee.*"

Photographs are not ordinarily permitted in utility patent applications. The USPTO will accept black and white photographs in utility patent applications only in applications in which the invention is not capable of being illustrated in an ink drawing or where the invention is shown more clearly in a photograph. Only one set of black and white photographs is required. Furthermore, no additional processing fee is required. Photographs have the same sheet size requirements as other drawings.

The photographs must be of sufficient quality so that all details in the drawing are reproducible in the printed patent or any patent application publication. Photographs must either be developed on double weight photographic paper or be permanently mounted on Bristol board. The photographs must be of sufficient quality so that all details in the drawing are reproducible in the printed patent. Color photographs will be accepted in utility patent applications if the conditions for accepting color drawings have been satisfied.

DRAWING REQUIREMENTS (Continued).

Identification of Drawings: Identifying indicia, if provided, should include the title of the invention, inventor's name, the application number (if known), the confirmation number (if known), and docket number (if any). This information should be placed on the top margin of each sheet of drawings, centered on the page. The name and telephone number of a person to call if the USPTO is unable to match the drawings to the proper application may also be provided.

Graphic Forms in Drawings: Chemical or mathematical formulas, tables, computer program listings, and waveforms may be submitted as drawings and are subject to the same requirements as drawings.

Each chemical or mathematical formula must be labeled as a separate figure, using brackets when necessary, to show that information is properly integrated. Each group of waveforms must be presented as a single figure, using a common vertical axis with time extending along the horizontal axis. Each individual waveform discussed in the specification must be identified with a separate letter designation adjacent to the vertical axis.

These may be placed in a landscape orientation if they cannot be presented satisfactorily in a portrait orientation. Typewritten characters used in such formulas and tables must be chosen from a block (nonscript) type font or lettering style having capital letters which are at least 0.21 cm. (0.08 inch) high (elite type). A space at least 0.64 cm. (1/4 inch) high should be provided between complex formulas or tables and the text.

DRAWING REQUIREMENTS (Continued).

Paper: Drawings submitted to the USPTO must be made on paper which is flexible, strong, white, smooth, nonshiny, and durable. All sheets must be free from cracks, creases, and folds. Only one side of the sheet shall be used for the drawing. Each sheet must be reasonably free from erasures and must be free from alterations, overwritings, and interlineations. All drawings sheets, including sheets containing photographs, in an application must be the same size. One of the shorter sides of the sheet is regarded as its top. The size of the sheets on which drawings are made must be one of two sizes:

- 21.6 cm. by 27.9 cm. (8 1/2 by 11 inches), or
- 21.0 cm. by 29.7 cm. (DIN size A4).

The sheets must not contain frames around the sight (the usable surface), but should have scan target points (cross hairs) printed on two catercorner margin corners. The following margins are required:

- On 21.6 cm. by 27.9 cm. (8 1/2 x 11 inch) drawing sheets, each sheet must include a top margin of at least 2.5 cm. (1 inch), a left side margin of at least 2.5 cm. (1 inch), a right side margin of at least 1.5 cm. (5/8 inch), and a bottom margin of at least 1.0 cm. (3/8 inch) from the edges, thereby leaving a sight no greater than 17.6 cm. by 24.4 cm. (6 15/16 by 9 5/8 inches).
- On 21.0 cm. by 29.7 cm. (DIN size A4) drawing sheets, each sheet must include a top margin of at least 2.5 cm. (1 inch), a left side margin of at least 2.5 cm. (1 inch), a right side margin of at least 1.5 cm. (5/8 inch), and a bottom margin of at least 1.0 cm. (3/8 inch) from the edges, thereby leaving a sight no greater than 17.0 cm. by 26.2 centimeter.

DRAWING REQUIREMENTS (Continued).

Views: The drawings must contain as many views as may be necessary to show the invention. The views may be plan, elevation, section, or perspective views. Detail views of portions of elements, on a larger scale if necessary, may also be used. All views of the drawing must be grouped together and arranged on the sheet(s) without wasting space, preferably in an upright position, clearly separated from one another and must not be included in the sheets containing the specifications, claims, or abstract. Views must not be connected by projection lines and must not contain center lines. Waveforms of electrical signals may be connected by dashed lines to show the relative timing of the waveforms.

***EXPLODED VIEWS*:** Exploded views, with the separated parts embraced by a bracket, to show the relationship or order of assembly of various parts are permissible. When an exploded view is shown in a figure which is on the same sheet as another figure, the exploded view should be placed in brackets.

***PARTIAL VIEWS*:** When necessary, a view of a large machine or device in its entirety may be broken into partial views on a single sheet, or extended over several sheets if there is no loss in facility of understanding the view.

Partial views drawn on separate sheets must always be capable of being linked edge to edge so that no partial view contains parts of another partial view. A smaller scale view should be included showing the whole formed by the partial views and indicating the positions of the parts shown. When a portion of a view is enlarged for magnification purposes, the view and the enlarged view must each be labeled as separate views.

DRAWING REQUIREMENTS (Continued).

PARTIAL VIEWS: (Continued). Where views on two or more sheets form, in effect, a single complete view, the views on the several sheets must be arranged that the complete figure can be assembled without concealing any part of any of the views appearing on the various sheets. A very long view may be divided into several parts placed one above the other on a single sheet. However, the relationship between the different parts must be clear and unambiguous.

SECTIONAL VIEWS: The plane upon which a sectional view is taken should be indicated on the view from which the section is cut by a broken line. The ends of the broken line should be designated by Arabic or Roman numerals corresponding to the view number of the sectional view, and should have arrows to indicate the direction of sight. Hatching must be used to indicate section portions of an object, and must be made by regularly spaced oblique parallel lines spaced sufficiently apart to enable the lines to be distinguished without difficulty. Hatching should not impede the clear reading of the reference characters and lead lines. If it is not possible to place reference characters outside the hatched area, the hatching may be broken off wherever reference characters are inserted.

Hatching must be at a substantial angle to the surrounding axes or principal lines, preferably 45°. A cross section must be set out and drawn to show all of the materials as they are shown in the view from which the cross section was taken. The parts in cross section must show proper material(s) by hatching with regularly spaced parallel oblique strokes, the space between strokes being chosen on the basis of the total area to be hatched.

DRAWING REQUIREMENTS (Continued).

SECTIONAL VIEWS: (Continued). The various parts of a cross section of the same item should be hatched in the same manner and should accurately and graphically indicate the nature of the material(s) that is illustrated in cross section. The hatching of juxtaposed different elements must be angled in a different way. In the case of large areas, hatching may be confined to an edging drawn around the entire inside of the outline of the area to be hatched. Different types of hatching should have different conventional meanings as regards to the nature of a material seen in cross section.

ALTERNATE POSITION: A moved position may be shown by a broken line superimposed upon a suitable view if this can be done without crowding; otherwise, a separate view must be used for this purpose.

MODIFIED FORMS: Modified forms of construction must be shown in separate views.

Arrangement of Views: One view must not be placed upon another or within the outline of another. All views on the same sheet should stand in the same direction and, if possible, stand so that they can be read with the sheet held in an upright position. If views wider than the width of the sheet are necessary for the clearest illustration of the invention, the sheet may be turned on its side so that the top of the sheet is on the right-hand side, with the appropriate top margin used as the heading space. Words must appear in a horizontal, left-to-right fashion when the page is either upright or turned so that the top becomes the right side, except for graphs utilizing standard scientific convention to denote the axis of abscissas (of X) and the axis of ordinates (of Y).

DRAWING REQUIREMENTS (Continued).

Front Page View: One of the views should be suitable for inclusion on the front page of the patent application publication and patent as the illustration of the invention.

Scale: The scale to which a drawing is made must be large enough to show the mechanism without crowding when the drawing is reduced in size to two-thirds in reproduction. Indications such as "actual size" or "scale 1/2" are <u>not</u> permitted on the drawings since these lose their meaning with reproduction in a different format.

Character of Lines, Numbers, and Letters: All drawings must be made by a process which will give them satisfactory reproduction characteristics. Every line, number, and letter must be durable, clean, black (except for color drawings), sufficiently dense and dark, and uniformly thick and well-defined. The weight of all lines and letters must be heavy enough to permit adequate reproduction. This requirement applies to all lines however fine, to shading, and to lines representing cut surfaces in sectional views. Lines and strokes of different thicknesses may be used in the same drawing where different thicknesses have a different meaning.

Shading: The use of shading in views is encouraged if it aids in understanding the invention and if it does not reduce legibility. Shading is used to indicate the surface or shape of spherical, cylindrical, and conical elements of an object. Flat parts may also be lightly shaded. Such shading is preferred in the case of parts shown in perspective, but not for cross sections. (Refer back to *sectional views*). Spaced lines for shading are preferred.

DRAWING REQUIREMENTS (Continued).

Shading: (Continued). These lines must be thin, as few in number as practicable, and they must contrast with the rest of the drawings. As a substitute for shading, heavy lines on the shade side of objects can be used except where they superimpose on each other or obscure reference characters. Light should come from the upper left corner at an angle of 45°. Surface delineations should preferably be shown by proper shading. Solid black shading areas are not permitted, except when used to represent bar graphs or color.

Symbols: Graphical drawing symbols may be used for conventional elements when appropriate. The elements for which such symbols and labeled representations are used must be adequately identified in the specification. Known devices should be illustrated by symbols which have a universally recognized conventional meaning and are generally accepted in the art. Other symbols which are not universally recognized may be used, subject to approval by the USPTO. If they are not likely to be confused with existing conventional symbols, and if they are readily identifiable.

Legends: Suitable descriptive legends may be used, or may be required by the Examiner, where necessary for understanding of the drawing, subject to approval by the United States Patent and Trademark Office. They should contain as few words as possible.

DRAWING REQUIREMENTS (Continued).

Numbers, Letters, and Reference Characters: The English alphabet must be used for letters, except where another alphabet is customarily used, such as the Greek alphabet to indicate angles, wavelengths, and mathematical formulas.

Reference characters (numerals are preferred), sheet numbers, and view numbers must be plain and legible, and must not be used in association with brackets or inverted commas, or enclosed within outlines (encircled). They must be oriented in the same direction as the view so as to avoid having to rotate the sheet. Reference characters should be arranged to follow the profile of the object depicted.

Numbers, letters, and reference characters must measure at least 0.32 cm. (1/8 inch) in height. They should not be placed in the drawing so as to interfere with its comprehension. Therefore, they should not cross or mingle with the lines. They should not be placed upon hatched or shaded surfaces. When necessary, such as indicating a surface or cross section, a reference character may be underlined and a blank space may be left in the hatching or shading where the character occurs so that it appears distinct.

The same part of an invention appearing in more than one view of the drawing must always be designated by the same reference character, and the same reference character must never be used to designate different parts.

Reference characters not mentioned in the description shall not appear in the drawings. Reference characters mentioned in the description must appear in the drawings.

DRAWING REQUIREMENTS (Continued).

Lead Lines and Arrows: Lead lines are those lines between the reference characters and the details to which they refer. Such lines may be straight or curved and should be as short as possible. They must originate in the immediate proximity of the reference character and extend to the feature indicated. Lead lines must not cross each other. Lead lines are required for each reference character except for those which indicate the surface or cross section on which they are placed. Such a reference character must be underlined to make it clear that a lead line has not been left out by mistake. Lead lines must be executed in the same way as lines in the drawing.

Arrows may be used at the ends of lines, provided their meaning is clear, as follows:

- On a lead line, a freestanding arrow to indicate the entire section towards which it points;

- On a lead line, an arrow touching a line to indicate the surface shown by the line looking along the direction of the arrow; or

- To show the direction of movement.

Copyright or Mask Work Notice: A copyright or mask work notice may appear in the drawing, but must be placed within the sight of the drawing immediately below the figure representing the copyright or mask work material and be limited to letters having a print size of 0.32 cm. to 0.64 cm. (1/8 to 1/4 inches) high. The content of the notice must be limited to only those elements provided for by law. (U. S. Copyright law, codes and regulations).

DRAWING REQUIREMENTS (Continued).

Copyright or Mask Work Notice: (Continued). For example, "©1983 John Doe" (17 U.S.C. 401) and "*M* John Doe" (17 U.S.C. 909) would be properly limited and, under current statutes, legally sufficient notices of copyright and mask work, respectively. Inclusion of a copyright or mask work notice will be permitted only if the authorization language set forth in 37 CFR §1.71(e) is included at the beginning (preferably as the first paragraph) of the specification.

Numbering of Sheets of Drawings and Views: The sheets of drawings should be numbered in consecutive Arabic numerals, starting with 1, within the sight (the usable surface). These numbers, if present, must be placed in the middle of the top of the sheet, but not in the margin. The numbers can be placed on the right-hand side if the drawing extends too close to the middle of the top edge of the usable surface. The drawing sheet numbering must be clear and larger than the numbers used as reference characters to avoid confusion.

The number of each sheet should be shown by two Arabic numerals placed on either side of an oblique line, with the first being the sheet number and the second being the total number of sheets of drawings, with no other marking. The different views must be numbered in consecutive Arabic numerals, starting with 1, independent of the numbering of the sheets and, if possible, in the order in which they appear on the drawing sheet(s). Partial views intended to form one complete view, on one or several sheets, must be identified by the same number followed by a capital letter. View numbers must be preceded by the abbreviation **FIG.**.

DRAWING REQUIREMENTS (Continued).

Numbering of Sheets of Drawings and Views: (Continued). Where only a single view is used in an application to illustrate the claimed invention, it must not be numbered and the abbreviation "FIG." must not appear. Numbers and letters identifying the views must be simple and clear and must not be used in association with brackets, circles, or inverted commas. The view numbers must be larger than the numbers used for reference characters.

Security Markings: Authorized security markings may be placed on the drawings provided they are outside the sight, preferably centered in the top margin.

Corrections: Any corrections on drawings submitted to the USPTO must be durable and permanent.

Holes: No holes should be made by the applicant in the drawing sheets. Rather than use of a staple, a non-hole producing binder clip should be used. (*End of Abbreviated Drawing Requirements*).

6). OATH OR DECLARATION The oath or declaration must identify the application to which it is associated, and must give the name, city, and either state or country of residence, country of citizenship, and mailing address of each inventor. It must state whether the inventor is a sole or joint inventor of the invention claimed. Additionally, designation of a correspondence address is needed on the oath or declaration. Providing a correspondence address will help to ensure prompt delivery of all notices, official letters, and other communications. In addition, a shortened declaration may be used in conjunction with an Application Data Sheet.

OATH OR DECLARATION (Continued). The oath or declaration must be signed by all of the actual inventors. An oath may be administered by any person within the United States, or by a diplomatic or consular officer of a foreign country, who is authorized by the United States to administer oaths. A declaration does not require any witness or person to administer or verify its signing. Thus, use of a declaration is preferable. The oath or declaration must be in a language which you understand. If the oath or declaration used is in a language other than English, the oath or declaration must either be (1) accompanied by a verified English translation, or (2) in a form provided or approved by the USPTO.

If the person making the oath or declaration is not the inventor, the oath or declaration shall state the relationship of that person to the inventor, upon information and belief, the facts which the inventor would have been required to state, and the circumstances which render the inventor unable to sign, namely death, insanity or legal incapacity or unavailability/refusal to sign. (See 37 CFR §1.42, 1.43, and 1.47). If the inventor has refused or cannot be reached to sign the declaration, then a petition under 37 CFR § 1.47 is required. (See 37 CFR § 1.47(b). For more information on signing for an inventor who cannot be reached or refuses to sign). If the inventor has died or is legally incapacitated, then the legal representative of the deceased or incapacitated inventor must sign the oath or declaration on behalf of the inventor.

7). SEQUENCE LISTING (When necessary). This section, for the disclosure of a nucleotide and/or amino acid sequence, should contain a listing of the sequence complying with 37 Code of Federal Regulations §1.821 through 37 Code of Federal Regulations §1.825 and may be in paper or electronic form.

Patents
NON-PROVISIONAL UTILITY PATENT APPLICATION

Well that about sums up the utility patent application regulations and drawing requirement. For more information, visit the USPTO website. Now here's an interesting story from an associate who followed a different path than mine. I am more of an idea, game and gimmick man. He's a developer of modern technology. President and CEO of Centerpin Technology, Inc., Rip Hanks discusses his trials and tribulations creating his company and it's products. "We at Centerpin have developed an easier way to terminate wire and cable. So our challenge as a company has been to protect, develop and bring to market this new innovation in electronics. Our strategy of building a strong patent portfolio has been the nucleus of our company. In my experience, the word "patent" offers a false sense of security to those who hold one. It did for us. We first started our company with an all encompassing utility patent that covered everything that related to a pin going into the end of a wire.

Or so I thought. After talking with large companies in efforts to license or sell our intellectual property, a sick feeling of reality over took me. The fact was I knew virtually nothing about patents, so my first order of business was to find someone who did. I located and brought on as a stockholder a recently retired litigation patent attorney from Chicago. I showed him our latest prototypes and animated video of our new products and asked him how he would get around our patent, if he were counsel for a large consumer electronics company. He told me that he didn't have to. The fact was that our patent claims didn't cover the new products at all. After the dizzying feeling of a living nightmare subsided, I asked him, 'How can we protect ourselves.' He told me that potentially our products could be protected under two new utility patents. That was the day I became a student of intellectual property. In the next couple of years we received two new utility patents which became the base of our intellectual property portfolio.

Patents

Our company model has been to become a licensing company like other sizable Electronic Laboratories. See Centerpins website **www.centerpin.com**. We license our technology to large companies in several industry categories and build our brand by requiring our trademarks to be displayed on products and packaging. We strive to improve our technology before someone else does. Today, we have 13 U.S. Utility Patents, 13 Foreign Patents and 14 U.S. and Foreign Trademarks. We sell 18 products in the marine industry under the Centerpin Brand and our licensed products have sold under RCA, Acoustic Research, Shakespeare Marine and Stinger Brands. The more successful your product is, the more resources a competitive company will be willing to allocate funds to find ways around your patent. If a product or technology is worth patenting, by all means find and hire a good patent attorney.

A good patent attorney is experienced in researching prior art (other patents), arguing for novelty over other patent claims and drafting claims to give the client the broadest coverage possible. Inventors sometimes think they are invincible and can do it all, including filing their own patent. My advice it is to harness the ego and hire a professional. Filing a patent without expertise in the area will leave the inventor wide open to a savvy patent attorney representing a competitor. The claims could be discredited or circumvented and weak research of prior art could result in a patent being rendered invalid. In my experience the better attorneys draft the claims first." I know my book is on patenting your idea yourself and it is possible, but as a amateur in the field of experts, can you be assured your own filing will protect you? As an inventor, you will be doing it yourself! Even with an attorney. You are paying him mostly as an advisor and protection expert. Seek out an attorney in the specialty field you are filing your patent under i.e.: If it's electrical, seek out a attorney familiar with electrical patent filings.

 **Requirements For Filing a**
DESIGN
Patent Application

Design patents may be granted to anyone who invents a new, original, and ornamental design for an article of manufacture. Design patents last 14 years from the date you are granted the patent. (No maintenance fees are required for design patents). A design patent protects only the appearance of the article and not structural or utilitarian features. A design consists of the visual ornamental characteristics embodied in, or applied to, an article of manufacture. A ornamental design may be embodied in an entire article or only a portion of an article, or may be ornamentation applied to an article. A "utility patent" protects the way an article is used and works, while a "design patent" protects the way an article looks. *Because design patents protect only the appearance of an article of manufacture, it is possible that minimal differences between similar designs can render each (design owned by two different inventors) patentable.*

Therefore, even though you may ultimately receive a design patent for your product, the protection afforded by such a patent may be somewhat limited. Both design and utility patents may be obtained on an article if the invention resides both in its utility and ornamental appearance. By providing your invention with a design and utility patent you will have greater protection than just a design patent alone. Many so-called Invention Development Organizations promise you a patent (which they cannot guarantee) on your idea or invention. Most likely, they will file for a design patent. Design patents are just that, patents on a design.

Patents

However, design patents are virtually worthless without a utility patent for protection. Why? Because with a design patent all I have to do is copy your invention and change it just slightly and file for my own design patent on your original idea. Note: Design patents do have a legal purpose and offer a small amount of protection so, consult legal counsel to see if it will offer enough protection for your creation. This story on obtaining a design patent comes from Bryon L. Woram and will help you understand the nominal amount of protection a design patent carries on inventions. "Having some time ago filed and been awarded a design patent for a golf club putter that allowed one to pick up the golf ball without bending over seemed, for all intent and purpose, to be a winning idea. The patent awarded me described the device as having a singular bore of specific diameter capable of affixing itself to a golf ball.

Additionally, the putter head is a mallet style, dimensioned in such a manner as to allow the putter to pick-up the ball after it had gone into the cup. Within six months of my patent approval, another patent pending approval was issued to someone for a putter of similar performance and released for sale onto the market. This new putter, upon request by me to my lawyer (expensively hired to protect my patent) requested and received a legal opinion from the infringing party's lawyer that described their design. Their determination was that their putter did not affix itself to the ball from the extreme outer edge of the bore but rather had a specific chamfer machined into the bore which allowed for the squeezing of a different and larger surface area of the golf ball, (they just machined the hole larger by a few fractions of an inch). Therefore, it did not infringe on my patent. After another costly discussion with my lawyer over litigation, I decided on a second opinion from another patent lawyer which cost me more money; and that lawyer agreed with everyone else.

From a layman's point of view, one could barely tell the difference between putters." This story you just read is true and should tell one that the design patent on an invention is perhaps not as important as a good marketing plan. Therefore, go for the patent, try to hold a patent pending position as long as possible (this makes it difficult for someone to take your idea and make it better) and plan to put a lot more time, money and effort into your marketing plan than the patent cost. So you can bring your product to market quicker. Quicker than the competition!

The elements of a design patent application should include the following:

(1) *PREAMBLE;* stating name of the applicant, title of the design, and a brief description of the nature and intended use of the article in which the design is embodied;

(2) *THE TITLE;*

(3) *THE FIGURE DESCRIPTIONS;*

(4) *A SINGLE CLAIM;*

(5) *DRAWINGS OR PHOTOGRAPHS;*

(6) *EXECUTED OATH OR DECLARATION.*

In addition, the filing fee set forth in 37 Code of Federal Regulations §1.16 (f) is also required. Fees are subject to change and should be double-checked on a current *Fee Schedule* before filing. Please note that two sets of fees exist, one for small entity (an independent inventor, a small business concern, or a non-profit organization) and one for other than small entity. If you meet the requirements of a small entity (and most likely you do as an independent inventor), the filing fee is reduced by half.

All of the previous elements are described below in numerical order. These descriptions are brief. View the complete application requirements online or order the guide directly from the USPTO.

1). THE PREAMBLE: The Preamble, if included, should state the name of the applicant, the title of the design, and a brief description of the nature and intended use of the article in which the design is embodied. All information contained in the preamble will be printed on the patent, should the claimed design be deemed patentable.

2). THE TITLE: The Title of the design must identify the article in which the design is embodied by the name generally known and used by the public. Marketing designations are improper as titles and should not be used. A title descriptive of the actual article aids the examiner in developing a complete field of search of the prior art. It further aids in the proper assignment of new applications to appropriate class, subclass, and patent examiner, as well as the proper classification of the patent upon allowance of the application. It also helps the public in understanding the nature and use of the article embodying the design after the patent has been published. Thus, applicants are encouraged to provide a specific and descriptive title.

3). THE FIGURE DESCRIPTIONS: The Figure Descriptions indicate what each view of the drawings represents, example, front elevation, top plan, perspective view, et cetera. Any description of the design in the specification, other than a brief description of the drawing, is generally not necessary since, as a general rule, the drawing is the design's best description. However, while not required, a special description is not prohibited.

In addition to the figure descriptions, the following types of statements are permissible in the specification:

- A description of the appearance of portions of the claimed design which are not illustrated in the drawing disclosure (i.e., "the right side elevational view is a mirror image of the left side").

- Description disclaiming portions of the article not shown, that form no part of the claimed design.

- Statement indicating that any broken line illustration of environmental structure in the drawing is not part of the design sought to be patented.

- Description denoting the nature and environmental use of the claimed design, if not included in the preamble.

4). A SINGLE CLAIM: A design patent application may only include a single claim. The claim defines the design which applicant wishes to patent, in terms of the article in which it is embodied or applied. The claim must be in formal terms to "The ornamental design for (the article which embodies the design or to which it is applied) as shown." The description of the article in the claim should be consistent in terminology with the title of the invention. When there is a properly included special description of the design in the specification, or a proper showing of modified forms of the design, or other descriptive matter has been included in the specification, the words "and described" should be added to the claim following the term "shown." The claim should then read "The ornamental design for (the article which embodies the design or to which it is applied) as shown and described."

5). DRAWINGS OR BLACK AND WHITE PHOTOGRAPHS:

The drawing disclosure is the most important element of the application. Every design patent application must include either a drawing or a black and white photograph of the claimed design. As the drawing or photograph constitutes the entire visual disclosure of the claim, it is of utmost importance that the drawing or photograph be clear and complete, that nothing regarding the design sought to be patented is left to conjecture. The drawings or photographs must include a sufficient number of views to constitute a complete disclosure of the appearance of the design claimed.

Drawings are normally required to be in black ink on white paper. Black and white photographs, in lieu of drawings, are permitted subject to the requirements of 37 CFR §1.84(b)(1) and §1.152. Applicant should refer to these rules. These rules set forth in detail the requirements for proper drawings in a design patent application.

Black and white photographs submitted on double weight photographic paper must have the drawing figure number entered on the face of the photograph. Photographs mounted on Bristol board may have the figure number shown in black ink on the Bristol board, proximate the corresponding photograph. Black and white photographs and ink drawings must not be combined in a formal submission of the visual disclosure of the claimed design in one application. Photographs submitted in lieu of ink drawings must not disclose environmental structure but must be limited to the claimed design itself. The guide for color drawings, color photographs, the views, broken lines, surface shading, design patent rules, along with disclosure examples can be viewed, or obtained by downloading: *A Guide to Filing A Design Patent Application* and *Patent Rules That Apply to Design Patent Applications* on the United States Patent and Trademark Office official website.

6). THE OATH OR DECLARATION: The oath of declaration required of the applicant must comply with the requirements set forth in 37 CFR §1.63.

The Design Patent Application Process: The preparation of a design patent application and the conducting of the proceedings in the USPTO to obtain the patent is an undertaking requiring the knowledge of patent law and rules and Patent and Trademark Office practice and procedures. A patent attorney or agent specially trained in this field is best able to secure the greatest patent protection to which the applicant is entitled. It would be prudent to seek the services of a registered patent attorney or agent. Representation, however, is not required. A knowledgeable applicant may successfully prosecute his or her own application.

However, while persons not skilled in this work may obtain a patent in many cases, there is no assurance that the patent obtained would adequately protect the particular design. Of primary importance in a design patent application is the drawing disclosure, which illustrates the design being claimed. Unlike a utility application, where the "claim" describes the invention in a lengthy written explanation, the claim in a design patent application protects the overall visual appearance of the design, "described" in the drawings. It is essential that the applicant present a set of drawings (or photographs) of the highest quality which conform to the rules and standards which are reproduced in the "The Guide to Filing A Design Patent Application." It is recommended that applicants retain the services of a professional draftsperson who specializes in preparing design patent drawings. When a complete design patent application, along with the appropriate filing fee, is received by the Office, it is assigned an Application Number and filing date. A "Filing Receipt" containing this information is sent to the applicant. The application is then assigned to an examiner.

Patents

"**MOON BRITCHES**" were originally created by Richard Cottrell, an entrepreneur who had great expectations for this line of clothing. (Created from an inspirational thought while cruising in his power boat). Richard is an avid water goer who from time to time came across other faster boats whose team on occasion would speed by MOONing his crew. As always, by the time they noticed the mocking sailors, it was too late to return the asinine (a little play on words) act. So he created a pair of shorts that could be unzipped in a short amount of time and facilitate the same showmanship. Well, word spread in the boating community and everyone wanted a pair of "Moon Britches." The trademark "Moon Britches" was applied for and the patent is still on going. Richard asked me for some help. So, I lent my creativeness to the concept and used a pair of cut-offs that had lycra sewn into them to print advertisements, and this increased sales.

You can see one of the several slogans featured in this picture here where I amused the audience wearing the "Moon Britches" during a promotional affair: "The Florida Bid For Bachelors," sponsored by the "American Cancer Society." Other slogans: "Rent This Space," "This Space For Lease" and more additional slogans were used for commercial advertising with larger firms. The possibilities are endless, and the advertising space increases with your waist size. (LOL).

Requirements For Filing a
PLANT
Patent Application

A plant patent is granted by the Government to an inventor (or the inventor's heirs or assigns) who has invented or discovered and asexually reproduced a distinct and new variety of plant, other than a tuber propagated plant or a plant found in an uncultivated state. This grant, which lasts for 20 years from the date of filing the application, protects the inventor's right to exclude others from asexually reproducing, selling, or using the plant so reproduced. This protection is limited to a plant in its ordinary meaning:

- A living plant organism which expresses a set of characteristics determined by its single, genetic makeup or genotype, which can be duplicated through asexual reproduction, but which can not otherwise be "made" or "manufactured."
- Sports, mutants, hybrids, and transformed plants are comprehended, sports or mutants may be spontaneous or induced. Hybrids may be natural, from a planned breeding program, or somatic in source. While natural plant mutants might have naturally occurred, they must have been discovered in a cultivated area.
- Algae and macro fungi are regarded as plants, but bacteria are not.

PROVISIONS AND LIMITATIONS

Patents to plants which are stable and reproduced by asexual reproduction, and not a potato or other edible tuber reproduced plant, are provided for by Title 35 USC, Section 161.

Whoever invents or discovers and asexually reproduces any distinct and new variety of plant, including cultivated sports, mutants, hybrids, and newly found seedlings, other than a tuber propagated plant or a plant found in an uncultivated state, may obtain a patent therefore, subject to the conditions and requirements of title. The provisions of this title relating to patents for inventions shall apply to patents for plants, except as otherwise provided.

As noted in the last paragraph of the statute of the previous page, the plant patent must also satisfy the general requirements of patentability. The subject matter of the application would be a plant, which has been developed or discovered by applicant, has been found stable by asexual reproduction. To be patentable, these would also be required:

- That the plant was invented or discovered and, if discovered, that the discovery was made in a cultivated area.

- That the plant is not a plant which is excluded by statute, where the part of the plant used for asexual reproduction is not a tuber food part, as with potato or Jerusalem artichoke.

- That the person or persons filing the application are those who actually invented the claimed plant; i.e., discovered or developed and identified or isolated the plant, and asexually reproduced the plant.

- That the plant has not been sold or released in the U.S.A. more than one year prior to the date of the application.

- That the plant has not been enabled to the public, example, by description in a printed publication in this country more than one year before the application for patent with an offer to sale, or by release or sale of the plant more than one year prior to application for patent with the USPTO.

- That the plant be shown to differ from known, related plants by at least one distinguishing characteristic, which is more than a difference caused by growing conditions or fertility levels, et cetera.

- The invention would not have been obvious to one skilled in the art at the time of invention by applicant.

Where doubt exists as to the patentability of a specific plant, a qualified legal authority should be consulted prior to applying to assure that the plant satisfies statutory requirements and is not exempted from plant patent protection.

Inventorship: Because there are two steps which constitute invention in plant applications, there may be more than one inventor. An inventor is any person who contributed to either step of invention. For example, if one person discovers a new and distinct plant and asexually reproduces the plant, such person would be a sole inventor. If one person discovered or selected a new and distinct plant, and a second person asexually reproduced the plant, and ascertained that the clone(s) of the plant were identical to the original plant in every distinguishing characteristic, the second person would properly be considered a co-inventor. If either step is performed by staff, every member of the staff who performed or contributed to the performance of either step could properly be considered a co-inventor. Thus, a plant patent may have a plurality of inventors. However, an inventor can direct that the step of asexual reproduction be performed by a custom propagation service or tissue culture enterprise and those performing the service would not be considered co-inventors.

Asexual Reproduction: Asexual reproduction is the propagation of a plant to multiply the plant without the use of genetic seeds to assure an exact genetic copy of the plant being reproduced.

Patents
PLANT PATENT APPLICATION

Any known method of asexual reproduction which renders a true genetic copy of the plant may be employed. Acceptable modes of asexual reproduction would include but may not be limited to these:

Rooting Cuttings/Apomictic Seeds/Division/Layering/Runners/ Tissue Culture/Grafting and Budding/Bulbs/ Slips/Rhizomes/Corms/Nucellar Embryos.

The purpose of asexual reproduction is to establish stability of the plant. This second step of the invention must be performed with sufficient time prior to application for patent rights to allow the thorough evaluation of propagules or clones of the claimed plant for stability, thus assuring that such specimens retain the identical distinguishing characteristics of the original plant.

Rights Conveyed by a Plant Patent: Grant of a patent for a plant precludes others from asexually reproducing or selling or using the patented plant. A plant patent is regarded as limited to one plant, or genome. A sport or mutant of a patented plant would not be considered to be of the same genotype, would not be covered by the plant patent to the parent plant, and would, itself, be separately patentable, subject to meeting the requirements of patentability. A plant patent expires 20 years from the filing date of the patent application. As with utility applications, when the plant patent expires, the subject matter of the patent becomes public domain.

Content and Arrangement: With some exceptions, a patent application for a plant is subject to the same requirements as a utility application. Title 37 CFR § 1.63(a) requires that the specification must contain as full and complete a botanical description as reasonably possible of the plant and the characteristics which distinguish that plant over known, related plants.

The components of a plant application are similar to those of a utility application and are covered by those guidelines which illustrate the preferred layout and content for patent applications. The guidelines suggested for use can be found on the USPTO website. There are no maintenance fees on plant patents.

Caution: The information provided in this book on plant patents is tailored to apply to and is limited to patents on asexually reproduced plants. While the USPTO does accept utility applications having claims to plants, seeds, genes, et cetera, such practice is beyond the scope of this information. General information regarding utility practice can be obtained by calling the PTO Information Services Division, or a registered patent attorney. Intellectual property protection for true breeding seed reproduced plant varieties is offered through the Plant Variety Protection Office Beltsville, Maryland, which should be contacted for information regarding intellectual property protection for such crops.

Most inventors would never think of a getting a plant patent, but how cool would it be? To find an unknown plant on a dark continent or just in your backyard and name it after yourself, your girlfriend, boyfriend, wife, husband, whom or whatever. So, for those who are lucky enough to find and produce a patentable plant, here's the correspondence information to help you.

Patent Assistance

Primary Examiners concerning the plant patent publication can be contacted at these phone numbers:

1-571-272-0980 / 1-571-272-0973 / 1-571-272-0974

Correspondence:
New patent applications should be mailed to:
Commissioner for Patents
P.O. Box 1450
Alexandria, VA 22313-1450

Requests for information regarding intellectual property protection for true breeding seed reproduced plant varieties is offered through:

Plant Variety Protection Office
Agricultural Marketing Service
National Agricultural Library Bldg. Room 0
10301 Baltimore Blvd.
Beltsville, Md. 20705-2351

COPIES OF PATENTS are furnished by the Patent and Trademark Office at $3.00 each; PLANT PATENTS in color, $15.00 each; copies of TRADEMARKS at $3.00 each. Address orders to:
The Commissioner of Patents and Trademarks,
P.O. Box 1450, Alexandria, VA., 22313-1450
(Fee Prices change so check with USPTO online or by telephone for exact cost).

For online ordering of patent forms and fees.
www.uspto.gov

Ask any question on patents, copyrights or trademarks at this website and you may get your question answered by an attorney.
www.lawguru.com

There are plenty of forums in this website below on intellectual property law, where other inventors ask questions and discuss issues. Check it out.
www.intelproplaw.com

Disclosure Document Program

A service provided by the USPTO is the acceptance and preservation for two years of "Disclosure Documents" as evidence of the date of conception of an invention. A paper disclosing an invention (called a Disclosure Document) and signed by the inventor or inventors may be forwarded to the United States Patent and Trademark Office by the inventor (or by any one of the inventors when there are joint inventors), by the owner of the invention, or by the attorney or agent of the inventor(s) or owner. The Disclosure Document will be retained for two years, and then be destroyed unless it is referred to in a separate letter in a related patent application filed within those two years.

These documents will be kept in confidence by the USPTO without publication in accordance with 35 U.S.C. 122(b) effective November 29, 2000. This program does not diminish the value of the conventional, witnessed, permanently bound, and page-numbered laboratory notebook or notarized records as evidence of conception of an invention, but it should provide a more credible form of evidence than that provided by the mailing of a disclosure document to oneself or another person by registered mail.

Content of the Disclosure Document
The benefits afforded by the Disclosure Document will depend directly upon the adequacy of the disclosure.

Disclosure Document Application

It is strongly recommended that the document contain a clear and complete explanation of the manner and process of making and using the invention in sufficient detail to enable a person having ordinary knowledge in the field of the invention to make and use the invention. When the nature of the invention permits, a drawing or sketch should be included. The use or utility of the invention should be described, especially in chemical inventions.

Preparation of the Disclosure Document
A standard format for the Disclosure Document is required to facilitate the USPTO's electronic data capture and storage. The Disclosure Document (including drawings or sketches) must be on white letter size (8.5 by 11 inch) or A4 (21.0 by 29.7 cm) paper, written on one side only, with each page numbered. Text and drawings must be sufficiently dark to permit reproduction with commonly used office copying machines. Oversized papers, even if foldable to the above dimensions, will not be accepted. Attachments such as videotapes and working models will not be accepted and will be returned.

Other Enclosures
The Disclosure Document must be accompanied by a separate cover letter signed by the inventor stating that he or she is the inventor and requesting that the material be received under the Disclosure Document Program. The inventor's request may take the following form:

"The undersigned, being the inventor of the disclosed invention,

requests that the enclosed papers be accepted under the

Disclosure Document Program, and that they be

Preserved for a period of two years."

Disclosure Document Application

When received

A notice with an identifying number and date of receipt in the United States Patent and Trademark Office will be mailed to the customer, indicating that the Disclosure Document may be relied upon only as evidence and that a patent application should be diligently filed if patent protection is desired. The USPTO prefers that applicants send two copies of the cover letter or Disclosure Document Deposit Request form and one copy of the Disclosure Document, along with a self-addressed stamped envelope. The second copy of the cover letter or form will be returned with the notice.

Warning to Inventors

The two-year retention period is not a "grace period" during which the inventor can wait to file his or her patent application without possible loss of benefits. It 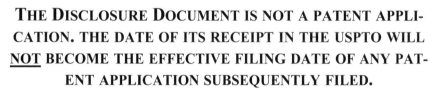 must be recognized that, in establishing priority of invention, an affidavit or testimony referring to a Disclosure Document must usually also establish diligence in completing the invention or in filing the patent application after the filing of the Disclosure Document.

THE DISCLOSURE DOCUMENT IS NOT A PATENT APPLICATION. THE DATE OF ITS RECEIPT IN THE USPTO WILL <u>NOT</u> BECOME THE EFFECTIVE FILING DATE OF ANY PATENT APPLICATION SUBSEQUENTLY FILED.

Inventors are also reminded that any public use or sale in the United States or publication of the invention anywhere in the world more than one year prior to the filing of a patent application on that invention will prohibit the granting of a United States patent on it. Foreign patent laws in this regard may be much more restrictive than United States of America laws.

Disclosure Document Application

Disposition

The Disclosure Document will be preserved in confidence by the USPTO for two years after its receipt without publication in accordance with 35 U.S.C. 122(b) effective November 29, 2000. It will be destroyed unless it is referred to in a separate letter in a related patent application filed within the two-year period. The separate letter filed in the related patent application must identify not only the patent application, but also the Disclosure Document by its title, number and date of receipt in the USPTO. Acknowledgement of such letters will be made in the next official communication or in a separate letter from the USPTO.

It is not necessary to submit more than one copy of the document in order for it to be accepted under the Disclosure Document Program although it is preferable to send two copies of the cover letter or one copy of the Disclosure Document Deposit Request form and one copy of the Disclosure Document. Send these along with a self-addressed stamped envelope. A Disclosure Document Deposit Request form (PTO/SB/95) can also be used as a cover letter. This form is available at the USPTO website or by calling the USPTO Contact Center.

The fee required is minimal (For current fees refer to the Fee Schedule at **www.uspto.gov** or call the USPTO Contact Center. Representatives can be reached from 8:30 AM to 8:00 PM Eastern Time, Monday through Friday (except Federal holidays).

<u>Mail your Disclosure Document with payment to</u>:

Mail Stop DD
Commissioner for Patents
P.O. Box 1450
Alexandria, VA 22313-1450

Disclosure Document Application

In an online discussion (**www.bpmlegal.com**) with Michael F. Brown (Registered Patent Attorney, no. 29,619), Mr. Brown gives his estimation on the Disclosure Document. "Referring to the old USPTO program where you can send anything at all to them with a small fee and they record it, supposedly to establish a date of conception for any utility application filed within two years. I do not approve of "Disclosure Documents." That program is both obsolete and useless. Worse than that, I have done extensive research on the subject, as have many other professionals I've discussed this with, and it is my opinion that filing a Disclosure Document is a Bad Idea for two reasons:

A. At best, the DD is useless for the purpose you would use the thing in the first place.

1) They were a favorite tool of unscrupulous Invention Marketing Companies for years because they were cheap and easy and misunderstood. The DD does not give the inventor a filing date or provide any other protection against people who filed afterward. Many inventors have been duped into sending these things into the PTO in the mistaken belief that they are then "protected," when they are not.

2) The most a DD can do is establish a date of conception for anything which is included in the filing. It cannot establish a date of invention, since invention requires both conception (coming up with the idea) and reduction to practice (building it or filing a patent application). In the extremely unlikely event that an interference is declared (less than 1% of applications, and much less than that if you exclude interferences between arguing co-inventors), you will have to prove conception and reduction to practice by hard evidence, and as long as you're doing that, an inventor's notebook or testimony of a third party is as good or better than the Disclosure Document, so why bother?

Disclosure Document Application

3) No one has been able to find, or has ever heard of, one single case where the DD was used to establish a date of invention in an interference or infringement case where priority of invention was an issue. Since these are the only situations in which the ostensible purpose of the DD would be served, clearly it is a waste of time.

4) The DD does not stop the "one year clock" of section 102(b) - that is, you have to file a patent application within a year of your first publication, public use or sale, and the DD is not a patent application. Too many people filed DD's, thinking that was a "patent document," sold their product, and then a year and a half later discovered that they could no longer file a patent application.

B. At worst, the DD can be harmful: I have found a number of cases in which badly written Disclosure Documents were used to limit the scope of the claims of the utility patent later issued. Thus, at worst, the DD is potentially damaging.

Bottom line, then - don't file Disclosure Documents. If you must file something preliminary, spend the extra money and file a Provisional Application which is as complete as you can possibly make it. The Provisional has the same (B) drawback as a DD - whatever you say in the Provisional may come back to bite you later, so you need to be very careful what you say - but at least you get a filing date and a date of invention, and the Provisional can provide a priority date against references which are published afterward."

For more on Disclosure Documents and other Patent Attorney related information go to Michaels website at **www.bpmlegal.com**. You can also view and print out his Invention Disclosure Form (Not to be confused with the USPTO Disclosure Document) which will help you organize your thoughts about your invention. View a partial of this form next, then visit his site to see the complete form.

Disclosure Document Application

Partial Invention Disclosure Form

- Name of Inventor(s):
- Name of Invention:
- Brief Description/Details of the Invention:
- Describe the invention in general terms: What does it do?
- How does it do it? What parts (steps, if a method) make up the invention, in its best (preferred) form?
- What does each contribute to the invention?
- Which parts are new to this invention (in form or usage), which are old (conventional, used in the expected way)?
- In what way do the parts interact to make the invention work?
- For each part, indicate if the part (or its form or interconnection) is ESSENTIAL to the invention - that is, for each part, ask, "if this part were left out, or changed, would the remaining device still be my invention?" Or, "if this part were changed or left out, would the invention still work?

If possible, use labeled sketches to detail your invention. Be sure all essential parts are shown on the sketch, and try not to include extraneous details. Measurements are not required, unless they are essential to the operation of the invention.

Note: A disclosure form of this type is used to disclose your invention to an attorney. In this case, Registered Patent Attorney Michael F. Brown who authorized use of this form for your viewing.

Non-Disclosure Agreement/Document

(NDA) is different from a disclosure document (DD). In a Disclosure Document the inventor discloses all his/her information to a certain party, in our case the USPTO, to establish the date of your idea's conception. A non-disclosure agreement (also known as a Confidentiality Agreement) is used when the inventor has an unpatented invention or idea and wants another party to view it and maintain any information disclosed in strict confidence.

Non-Disclosure Document

It protects the disclosing party who reveals his/her idea as confidential information. Now let's talk more about the NDA; if you insist on confidentiality when trying to market your invention to corporations or manufacturers, do not be surprised if they emphasize they will not see your product in confidence. That is, they will not sign your non-disclosure agreement. I have insisted throughout this book before showing your invention or discussing your idea with anyone, make sure they sign your NDA. Well always insist, but its more than a 80% chance they will turn you down; and if you maintain a paranoia of someone stealing your idea and insisting on them signing a NDA, you just lost out on a large percentage of companies who may have been valuable prospects. Even the best NDA ever written still may not be enough protection if you don't have the finances to enforce it.

If you are going to be concerned about someone stealing your idea, you are going to scare away possible investors and never get the assistance you need. Safekeeping your invention or idea is a legitimate concern to the inventor, but when seeking help with your finances, you are going to have disclose your information. When seeking investors or licensing agreements you cannot act paranoid of disclosing your product or prototype, you may scare off a potential sponsor of your invention. So, if your paranoid, get the protection you need with a provisional patent application. This will end your fear and you can show your product in confidence and state it's patent pending. You can also visit a site that prides itself on being the most advanced provider of automated legal documents on the internet. Their staff and legal team research legislation throughout the United States and the Commonwealth to update their documents into full compliance. Their easy-to-use, step-by-step approach makes it uncomplicated for the inventor to obtain legal documents such as: Confidentiality/Non-Disclosure Agreements. For more information visit their website at **www.Lawdepot.com**.

Disclosure Document Assistance

To Receive a Disclosure Document Deposit Request form which can also be used as a cover letter, request form, **PTO/SB/95**, or go online to the website, look for the search box, and type it in.

USPTO Website: **www.uspto.gov**
USPTO Contact Center: 1-800-786-9199 or 1-703-308-4357
USPTO Contact Center: Fax number: 1-571-273-3245
USPTO Contact Center: TTY 1-703-305-7785

The Inventors Assistance Center (IAC) provides patent information and services to the public. The IAC is staffed by former Supervisory Patent Examiners and experienced Primary Examiners who answer general questions concerning patent examining policy and procedure. Address: Mail Stop 24

Director of the U.S. Patent and Trademark Office
P.O. Box 1450
Alexandria, VA 22313-1450

Telephone: 1-800-786-9199   Fax: 1-703-306-5570
TTY 1-703-305-7785

E-mail: **independentinventor@uspto.gov**

The Texas Intellectual Property Partnership (TIP2) participates as USPTO's authorized "agent" in accepting documents filed under the Disclosure Document Program. This service provides a completed transaction on-site. Documents receive an identifying number and date at the time of receipt by the PTDL. Original documents are sent to the USPTO for processing and retention, at:

Texas A & M University Libraries
Sterling C. Evans Library Annex—MS 5000
College Station, TX 77843-5000
Phone: 1-979-458-1819
E-mail: **TIP2@lib-gw.tamu.edu**

Other Patent and Trademark Depository Libraries can be found online at the USPTO website.

SUNSHINE SURFBOARD COMPANY

1968 "Shark's Pit"
South Florida.

Vic-Vincent's first small company was manufacturing and selling surfboards at age 15. Shown above left, this surfboard was the smallest manufactured in the United States.
By Sunshine Surfboards, it was 5'6".
The next smallest surfboard in the U.S. at that time was 10'6".

Chapter Eight
Making a Company

Let's start by creating a company image to look and sound **BIG-GER** than we really are. We already have a great name for our company. Let's say "Vic-Vincent!" Well, that's not very impressive by itself, and it sounds as if only one person is running the whole show. Everyone can see through that no matter how impressive we sound. We are trying to persuade people into thinking we own a large company, not a one person show, so they feel we've been in business a long time, and they feel comfortable doing business with us. So we could add Company, Productions, or Group anything that adds status to our name. Now, let's see, "Vic-Vincent Corp." Much, much better! (Legally; Corp. or Corporation can be added only if you incorporate).

Now, it seems as though more than one person is working with me. Well, we've got our name straightened out. Now let's enlarge our business so we look and sound impressive. You may say, give me a call at the office when you look over my literature. Uh-Oh! Big mistake, your client calls and you answer the phone. How big does your company seem now? (This is one reason you may want your company to have a name other than your own). There's several things you can do. **First**, you can muffle your voice, and say "Vic-Vincent Corporation. Hold on please. I'll connect you," but that's pretty risky. Almost anyone can tell you are trying to fake being a receptionist unless you can disguise your voice very well.

Making a Company

The **second** thing you can do is buy a phone that changes your voice, but for the most part, these phones sound very robotic. If you do get one of these voice changers, make sure you have a friend call in and listen to you so you can set the right voice level and don't end up sounding like a munchkin! **Three,** I have found getting an answering service is best. They are very professional, and they will say whatever you would like them to say, "I'm sorry, he's in a meeting," "He's gone to lunch," "He left for Washington D.C. this morning, but he is checking his messages every two hours. May I have your name and number, so he can call you back?" Then you call them back, as if you are calling from Washington. It makes your clients feel important, as if you went out of your way to call them. **Fourth,** use an answering machine to take calls when you are away. Record your outgoing message using background noises, like people working in a warehouse and say, "we are closed for inventory, please leave a message," or be very creative and say this:

"Hello, I am away from my car right now, but my calls are being transferred back to my office, please leave a message at the sound of the tone." I like that one! **Fifth,** there is a digital message center you can buy that will make you seem like you work in the empire state building. This machine can take messages for different departments or employees and begin with a style of message that lets you choose a number of options to leave a voice message with: "to speak with Mr. Vic-Vincent, press #1; if you would like to speak with Steve in sales, press #2. This way callers can leave a message for the recipient personally. You could also do this yourself more cheaply by using an answering machine and say, "You have reached the Vic-Vincent Corporation. If you would like to speak to someone in shipping, press #1. If you would like to speak to someone about our products, press #2. Sales, press #3." "I'm sorry, no one is available right now, you may leave your message with voice mail and someone will return your call.

Making a Company

Thank you. Leave your message at the sound of the beep!" Beep! **Sixth**, you can purchase a phone with a hold button and always answer your phone with your company name. When they ask for you, just say, "please hold." Then, put them on hold, wait a few seconds, pick up, and say your name and "may I help you." It's so quick they won't recognize your voice. **Seventh**, the phone company now has voice mail you can use for a small monthly fee that acts as a digital voice message center. This is more business-like than an answering machine and is worth the cost. You can access your messages from anywhere, anytime. While we are on the subject of telephones, let's talk about the yellow pages. Listing your company in the phone book can be very expensive. If you do not have to have a listing, don't. Just use your residence listing because a business listing requires a higher billing rate and in most cases a separate telephone line.

If you have to have a business listing in the phone book, just use the standard company listing, no extras, no fancy ads. Ads are very expensive, cost monthly, and if you get no return from your ad, you can't drop the ad for one year until the new phone books are published. If you think you can get out of paying for your ad, you can't. The phone company will disconnect your phone and any future business will be lost. Also, try to list under separate headings if possible, so you are the only one, Ex: **Vic-Vincent Game Company**. I put this listing under wholesale manufacturers. Not that many companies listed under this heading like they did for just "Games." When the ad went in under the city my business was in, I ended up being the only one listed under wholesale manufacturers, so my name stood out from all the rest. It looked as though I was one of the biggest game companies in that area, and it didn't cost me any more to get my own separate line or heading. Here's a couple of suggestions for listing your company in the telephone directory, especially if you are in a service type business, like heating and air.

Making a Company

There are several large companies in this field listed in the yellow pages, most with big expensive ads. These companies rely on their reputation and the clientele they have built up over the years to bring them repeat business. They do very well at it, and their ads bring them new customers consistently. They even have sales representatives who sell their products and promote their business. That's how they are able to afford those ads. So, how do we compete? We create a company name that comes before all the other heating and air conditioning companies in the telephone directory. If their names start with a B or V we can get listed in the phone book by using a name that starts with an A, like, "Acme." So, we use the alphabet! All listings are not on a first come, first serve basis. They are in alphabetical, numerical order, so let's be sneaky and call ourselves "A Touch of Gold Heating and Cooling." Now, considering no one is using this name, we may be first in the phone book under this classification.

It didn't cost us any extra, and, when people have trouble with their a/c, most likely, they will start at the first listing in the phone book. Keep in mind you must show proof that you are using this name with an "A" in it, such as a business license. When you go to have it listed and someone is listed under, "AAA Air-conditioning Service." Just be a little trickier, use "AA Air-conditioning." The listings start with A (and a space, then a number. Example: A 24 Hour Company. The order of alphabetical-numerical listings in the phone book can be very complex. So, check with the phone company because there are also some listings that I have left out that may be inserted before some of these, depending on your letter and number structure, such as A & A, A-B, A-1, AB&C et cetera. Also check the listings in your area, under your category, to see the sequence of alpha-numerical arrangements, so you can be sure you are not copying someone else's name, and you can still be creative and be the first under your heading.

Making a Company

If you believe you are in a specialized field and you have no competition, you may want to use a gimmick name because you will be the only one under your profession or business, such as Zebra Animal Painting. In this case, it's most likely you are the only animal painter in town, so you don't have to have a company name such as Animal Painters to be first in the phone book. Your gimmick name will do and may even bring you more attention. Also, get caller I.D. and call waiting so you don't miss any calls if your on the other line, and if you do miss a call you can check your caller identification readout. These are just a few of your options. Now, that's the phone company's listings. Let's talk about phone numbers. Try to get a phone number that's easy to remember like 111-game or 222-toys. Take a list of your own numbers and letters with you when you go to the telephone company and hand them to the representative.

They can check them on their computer for you and if all of those numbers are unavailable, ask to see a computer run of the unused phone #'s that you can pick from. If you are not using a gimmick phone #, such as a name, then use a number that's easy to remember, like 111-1111, a number that your customers or clients don't always have to look up in the phone book. Just keep asking for unused #'s until you get satisfaction, and, if you still do not get one you are happy with, come back another day. The listings change almost daily and this will give you time to ponder your phone number and how you want it listed. Make sure you are happy with your phone number because all your company stationery, business cards, websites et cetera, will have this number imprinted on it, and it will be very costly to change it later. If you do change it later and you have a lot of out-of-town clients that do not call you that often, they will have to be notified of your telephone number change or you could lose customers. O.K., now you've got your name, phone book listing and phone number; you need an address.

Making a Company

If you are thinking about starting up a business and don't already own a home and the place you are renting has a name like, Three Cats and a Dog apartment complex, I would suggest you think about moving to another location like an apartment or condominium complex that's called "Park Place" or "Boardwalk," and this will add a little more clout to your over all business address, like this:

Vic-Vincent Corp.
Boardwalk, Suite-0
0000 Bluebird Lane
Gulf Breeze, Florida 32561

<u>Notice:</u> I added suite instead of using condo unit or a apartment number, which sounds like I have a great commerce establishment when actually I'm working out of my rat-infested, one-room apartment. (LOL).

The postal service may require you to use condo or apartment, but maybe you can get by using Townhouse or Estates. Probably, the only mandatory reasoning would be if there were two Boardwalk complexes; then you would have to use the correct heading to make sure you get your mail. But no matter, there are a lot of condos being used as offices now-a-days, and it is getting to where most small businesses work out of their homes, so it's not as looked down upon as it once was. If most people had their choice, I am sure they would rather work at home. Now, maybe we like where we are living, but we are not sure how long we will be there; then, a P.O. Box is your answer, and it's very safe. No matter how many times you move, your P.O. Box will remain the same, but it will be in the same city you placed it in, so don't move too far! Also, when using a P.O. Box, it will never matter where you do your business from because they will never know, and you can always have your mail forwarded even if you do move.

Making a Company

We could be working out of our car! It doesn't matter where we live or where we work, our mail will always be sent to the P.O. Box. One option for a very good address is to look for mail forwarding companies that allow you to use their address, such as "The World Trade Tower," "The Sears Tower," or "The Empire State Building." These are just a few examples that may or may not be available, but they surely are impressive! Mail forwarders allow you to use their address and then forward your mail to you. Again, your associates will never have to know where you live or work. Example:

Vic-Vincent Corp.
362 Gulf Breeze Pkwy.
Suite 151
Gulf Breeze, Fla. 32561

Vic-Vincent Corp.
Empire State Building
Suite A-110
New York, N.Y. 01111

Obviously, the Empire State Building address is incorrect, but these are just examples to show you the impact of certain addresses. The Post Office requires you to use the designation P.O. Box if you have one, but I use the # sign in my address instead of the words P.O. Box and I still get my mail.

Vic-Vincent Publishing
362 gulf breeze pkwy. #151
Gulf Breeze, FL 32561

We have our name, our phone number, our phone number listing, and address; now, we need a business card with this information to attract customers. You're in business, so make your card look like it. Stay away from black and white; instead, use bright colors, raised letters, gold foil printing, maybe even a different cut to the old rectangular shape. Make it round, shape it like an airplane, anything, just make it different. Why? Because almost every business person I know gets a lot of business cards every day, and they just get filed away, most filed straight into the trash can.

Making a Company

So maybe, just maybe, if it's different, they'll keep it, and when they go to look for it among all the other cards, they can find it easier and faster since its more noticeable because of that funny shape or color! Business cards are not that expensive, but it's one of your most important business tools. When you meet perspective clients, sometimes you don't have that much time to discuss business, so you give them your card, so that they can call you back later to talk or set up a meeting. Now, you've talked with them, and you want to keep in touch without being a pest. Write them a letter using pre-printed letterheads with your company name and address on your stationery, or use your computer to make a pre-programmed company heading. A printing company can do a very nice job for your business stationery, plus make up pre-printed envelopes to match. If you want to be really creative, you can create your own company logo and the printers can add this to your business cards, stationery, and envelopes.

If you make them all to match, this will give you a very good first impression. None of this is very costly, and it will look very professional. If you want a certain color, say red for example, ask the printers what day they will be using red and you probably can get a discount, rather than making an exclusive order. When you think you have everything in order to start your business, you find out you are just beginning. Now comes the legal paperwork. Everyone wants a piece of the action, that includes the city, the county, the state, even the federal government. Before you purchase a license to do business in your area, make sure local ordinances do not prohibit businesses from working out of a residential area. Next, you need to get a tax I.D. number if you have employees. Then, you need to decide whether or not you want to create a sole proprietorship, partnership, or a corporate structure.

All have certain advantages and disadvantages.

Making a Company

A SOLE PROPRIETORSHIP is often the way to go in the beginning. More than seventy-percent of all small businesses are sole proprietorships. You have no bosses or partners to worry about, and you keep all the profits. Accounting is very simple if kept on a cash basis and taxes (business losses or gains) are included on the owners personal income tax return. However, if you have created something that may cause you a lawsuit, then you may want to contact a corporation attorney because, in a sole proprietorship, you are liable if your product causes any harm or injury, and you could lose your home and all your possessions.

PARTNERSHIPS are started when one or more persons decide they want to enter a business relationship together. They each become owners of the business and share responsibilities. They each agree on terms on the amount of time and capital each colleague will invest and, most importantly, the amount of profits each partner will share. In a partnership, it must be clear what each person's job description is. To avoid any misinterpretation of each investor's authority and responsibilities, you should have legal documents drawn up by an attorney. This may sound excessive to a small operator, but, believe me, it is not. Anytime a business involves more than one person who has authority, you must make it clear what each person's responsibility is. You must make up a Partnership Agreement to protect all parties. In a partnership, arguments are sure to arise, and the only recourse to solve these arguments may be your agreement. There could be major changes in your company such as a partner wanting to retire or a question of who pays what share of liability in a legal dispute, even trivial problems such as who cleans the office windows or bathroom. If these questions and more are not answered before you enter into a partnership, your whole company could be dissolved in the future over any number of disagreements. With a partnership agreement, most of your problems can probably be avoided.

Making a Company

If you have a legal document made up on each partner's responsibilities, then you will be able to resolve most disputes that arise. Have a legal agreement prepared by a corporation attorney. They are very familiar with all aspects of big and small businesses and can help you with many things you may overlook in trying to write your own contract of responsibilities. I had an idea for a new business that I didn't have capital for, so I took on a partner who could invest in this start-up company. I just assumed as a partner each knew they were responsible fifty percent. Well, the investor's fifty percent was just capital. I did one-hundred percent of the work and the investor collected fifty percent of the profit. Needless to say, this arrangement lasted only six months.

There were too many disagreements we could not resolve. I was so happy to find an investor in my business that I didn't stop to think about what each person's responsibilities would be. We ended up arguing over almost everything because we never had an understanding of what was expected of the  other, so I dissolved our partnership by closing the business. All of this could have been avoided had I taken the time to write an agreement. The upside to taking on a partner is the advantage of using each other's knowledge to make decisions and the extra capital a partner brings with him or her that's needed to run a business before it's profitable. Another plus is taxes are shared by the individual partners.

NEVER ASSUME ANYTHING! GET IT IN WRITING!

Making a Company

In a **CORPORATION**, the members and shareholders are a separate entity from the company. The advantage of a corporation is that it can be sued for damages, but you are protected as a stock holder and cannot be touched personally. Also, if a stock holder wants out of the company, all he or she has to do is sell all his or her stock. With this in mind, co-owners can come and go as they please without dissolving the company. You can also sell company stock, common or preferred, to raise funds. A disadvantage is that you are taxed twice: on yourself and your company, unlike a sole proprietorship where you are only taxed once on your income.

In a **S CORPORATION**, you can maintain big corporation status but with fewer headaches. With an S Corporation shareholders include income and losses on their individual tax return. There are certain requirements that must be met, but it's great for the small business person. It allows you the protection of a corporation and the advantages of a partnership.

In a **LIMITED LIABILITY COMPANY**, this type of business brings together some of the best features of corporations and partnerships. Business owners enjoy the liability protection like that of large corporations and also avoid double taxation. It is the better of all entities for tax purposes. Earnings and losses are passed on to the owners then included on their personal tax returns. Treatment of LLC's vary in each state when it comes to taxes, if you decide on a LLC structure meet with a CPA who can explain the rules and regulations.

To find out more information on small business tax laws, call a local Internal Revenue Service office. Then pick up your free booklet called "Tax Guide for Small Business" (Publication 334), or go online at **www.irs.gov**. Bookkeeping may be a little tricky at first, but it's not really all that difficult. Have someone in another small business show you how he or she manages his or her books.

Making a Company

Ask the owners what licenses are required to operate their business. Then verify it when you go to the proper offices for licenses, et cetera. Let's round this up: Get a Sellers Permit and Sales Tax I.D. number. (So you won't have to pay sales tax when you buy products for your business or pay tax on out of state sales). If you plan to start a business such as a restaurant, you will have to check on county health codes. If you plan to open a pawn or antique shop, you will need a permit from the police department. Purchase a business license and file a fictitious name for your business at the county clerk's office. Decide whether or not you want to be a Sole Proprietorship, Partnership, or Corporation. Ask for help. Be Legal! Funding for our business can come from many different sources. I have listed several below to choose from.

Tax Refund / Small Business Admin. / Family Loan / Venture Capital Firms / Savings and Loans / Relatives / Refinance Auto / Sell Personal Items / 401k Retirement Loan / Your Savings / Commercial Bank Loan / Personal Bank Loan / Bank Collateral Loan / Credit Union Loan / Investors / Partners / Shareholders / Home Equity Loan.

Before seeking any type of capital, you need to figure out what your costs will be to produce your product and what your expenses will be to successfully sustain your business for at least twelve months, which is normally the time of your initial lease of an office space. First time entrepreneurs always make the common mistake of trying to figure minimum investment costs, leaving out important items such as insurance, licenses, deposits, utilities and many small things that add up, such as shipping costs. Office costs such as phones, faxes, and computers are often overlooked. Don't try to underestimate to just get by; this could easily bankrupt you quickly. Don't start what you cannot finish! Make sure you have enough capital to at least give your dream a chance of surviving.

Making a Company

Check State and Federal Regulations

If you are in the business of food preparation, drugs, cosmetics, flammables, et cetera, there are state and federal regulations you must comply with. There are also guidelines to follow if you have a service or environmental business, such as oil recycling. If you are in doubt about your product or business, call the state and federal agency about your particular business. The Department of Revenue can help you with information on the regulations regarding taxation and licensing. Businesses with employees are affected by regulations controlling working conditions, wages, et cetera. Contact the Dept. of Labor. If you decide to become a corporation or a limited partnership, you must be granted this by the state. See a corporate attorney. The charge is usually under five-hundred dollars and he or she will give you a better understanding of corporate law. For the do-it-your-selfers, fill out the forms yourself. Contact the State Division of Corporation for information or check with your local office supplier for legal forms under "Incorporation."

Check City and County Regulations and Licensing

If the business is located within an incorporated city limits, you must obtain a occupational license from the city; if outside the city limits, you must obtain one from the county. Register with the city clerk and the county tax collector for each location your company will be doing business in. If you are unincorporated, you must comply with The Fictitious Names Act and register through the Division of Corporations of the Department of State. Check with your local newspapers to see if they publish a fictitious name section. Sometimes they will do the paperwork for you. Cost is usually around fifty dollars. If your business is registered in your exact name, then you will not have to comply with the Fictitious Name Act. Other regulations to consider in your local area are fire prevention, police, health, building, and zoning codes.

Making a Company

Hiring Employees

Job services or employment agencies in your state can find adequate employees skilled in your type of business for you. Some states have a Private Industry Council that provides training for employees and can even help with the subsidizing of their wages for on the job training. Employees can make or break a company with attitudes, theft, and lazy work habits. So, do a thorough interview; check their references and past employment history. Along with employees, you have a whole new set of regulations you must abide by. These include Worker's Compensation Insurance, Social Security Tax, Unemployment Tax et cetera. For state and federal laws, I suggest you seek counsel from the SBA or a corporate attorney.

Locating Your Business

I also suggest as a start-up company, if you can work out of your home, then do so. Having no major overhead costs is a tremendous relief and may even be a tax deduction (see your tax accountant, or call the IRS). If you're planning to sell retail (commercially) and have a unique product, your customers will come to you, so location may not be that important. If you are not so lucky, then consider where your customers shop and locate there. To help you with the demographics of your business, contact the SBA. They can help you identify your market with regard to customers and locations.

Licenses

State licensing is required for certain businesses such as building and electrical contractors. Most likely, this does not pertain to you, but, if in doubt, call The State Department of Professional Regulations. Almost every city and county requires an occupational license. (See city and county regulations and licensing).

Making a Company

Taxes

There are so many different types of taxes that you will have to become familiar with when you start your own business. I will list many here, but to be sure you are paying the proper taxes associated with your business, call the IRS and discuss the type of business you are setting up; and they will guide you in the right direction. Remember it may all seem overwhelming at first, but as time goes by, you will get the hang of it; and remember everyone in business has to pay taxes, so don't feel they are just after you. I know when I originally opened my first business, I couldn't believe all the requirements I had to comply with to become operational. Licenses, taxes, regulations, everyone wanted a piece of me. Well I got madder and madder and so will you, but I am hear to tell you, your going to have to get over it and just comply if you want to become an entrepreneur: the sooner the better. There are almost 19 million small businesses, so you are not alone. There are at least 18,999,999 other mad people out there. It's just part of the process you will have to endure, and maybe in the long run, you will have to pay lots of taxes which means you will be making lots of money. Here's a little of what I am talking when it comes to the different types of taxes:

Federal Taxes	Self Employment Tax	Income Tax
County Tax	Employment Tax	State Taxes
Sales & Use Tax	Tangible Personal Property Tax	Real Property Tax
Sales & Gross Receipts Tax	Specialized Business Tax	Unemployment Tax
City Tax	Social Security Tax	Excise Tax

Making a Company Check List

Check Off Each Line As You Accomplish It.

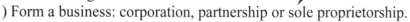

) Create a company name.
) Create a company logo, if you desire.
) File for trademark protection of your company
  name and logo.
) Form a business: corporation, partnership or sole proprietorship.
) Check zoning laws for your business location. Call city inspector.
) Create a place for business: home, office, garage, et cetera.
) Locate an address for business: P.O. Box, home, condo, et cetera.
) Obtain business insurance protection.
) File for your business occupational license.
) File for a fictitious name.
) File for a sales tax permit and receive your sales tax I.D. number.
) File for federal EIN (employer identification number) if needed.
  (Form SS-4).
) Print up your business cards and stationery.
) Have a telephone connected under your company name.
) Hire sales people, employees (if necessary).
) Hire an accountant if needed.
) Secure funds: venture capital, loans, personal financing.
) Open a bank account in your company name.
) Create a company website.
) Contact printers (for copies of sales material et cetera).
) Start advertising.
) Get publicity.

Seek help through the (SBA) or (SCORE).

See if your state has a "*State Product Development Center*" to aid small businesses. Look in your state's capital blue pages of the phone book.

Network with other entrepreneurs, join the
Chamber of Commerce.

Making a Company Assistance

Small Business Administration: (SBA)
www.sba.gov
Telephone: 1-800-827-5722
Every state has at least one SBA district office. Their mission is to aid, counsel, assist and protect the interests of small businesses. Go online and search their database for the office nearest you and good small business advice.

Service Corps of Retired Executives: (SCORE)
www.score.org
In the search box of this site menu, type in SCORE for a phone number, e-mail address and location nearest you. Call them and be prepared to give them information on yourself and your project so they can select a counselor to meet your needs.

Internal Revenue Service: (IRS)
www.irs.gov
Live Telephone Assistance: 1-800-829-1040
Live Telephone Assistance for Businesses: 1-800-829-4933
Live Telephone Assistance for Hearing Impaired: 1-800-829-4059

U.S. Chamber of Commerce:
www.uschamber.com
Go online and search their database for a local chapter near you.
Main Number: 1-202-659-6000
Customer Service: 1-800-638-6582

U.S. Government Business Link:
www.business.gov
Excellent site. I suggest you go here and complete the startup business checklist. This will give you a very good idea of how and what you will need to prepare for starting your own business. Go to the Business Homepage. Click on Launching. Click on Are You Ready? Click on Checklist for Starting A Business. This will guide and prepare you for self employment.

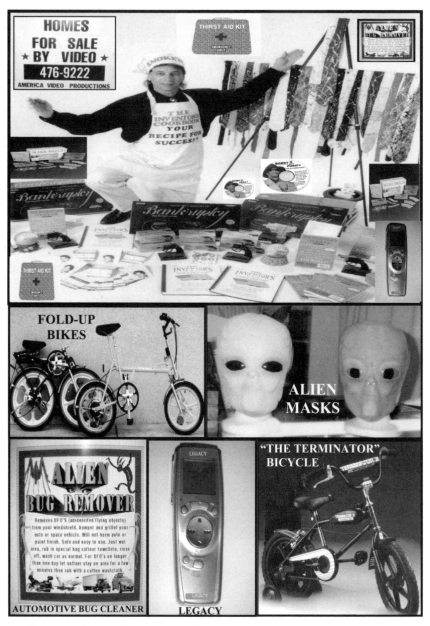

Companies and products (his and others) Vic-Vincent was involved with in sales, marketing and production.

Chapter Nine
Producing Your Product With Manufacturers

You've finished all your preliminary steps; now you need to produce your product for retail. Get several manufacturers to give you price quotes, but don't necessarily go for the cheapest manufacturer without researching the company or the person. Sometimes, the quotes are lower with one manufacturer than another with the same materials, but that company may not be able to produce your product as fast as the other. For start-ups, if you are satisfied with the time it will take to produce the items and the quality of the item itself, time may not matter to you, and the cheapest way out is always the most important, at least on your initial budget.

We can always produce a more sophisticated version of our product after it becomes a hit! (Many large companies produce products on a low budget just to test the market). The reason one company can produce your item at a lower price and another company cannot is most likely that the other company needs your business. So talk with someone at the company that needs your business and negotiate. In the start-up phase of our product, we will want the quality as high as possible, but, if you build your product with gold instead of plastic, you can't afford to make it, and how many people can afford to buy it? Keep it as simple as possible. We want the general public to be able to afford it and to buy it!

Producing Your Product With Manufacturers

If you produce your creation cheaper than the competition, there are more smaller stores that may carry your product rather than just a few expensive retail stores. Sometimes, the manufacturers can show you ways to cut your costs. The manufacturers may be able to lower your costs by using different materials, other than the materials you are using now. You also need to think into the future when choosing a manufacturer. If your product becomes an overnight success, you may have to produce your products fast, and it's more likely that the bigger companies can produce faster and cheaper on larger orders. Keep all this in mind when you are shopping for a manufacturer. Continue to go back and forth with all the manufacturing companies you received quotes from to tell them what the others will produce your product for. In fact, go to the one who puts out quality products and is the fastest and most reliable.

Try to get this manufacturer to lower his or her quote. Show this manufacturer what the other company offered to make your product for, and most likely if this manufacturer wants or needs your business, he or she will lower the bid! If the manufacturer is in great demand and shows no willingness to lower the cost, then maybe he or she can produce an extra hundred or so of your product for free. If the manufacturer shows no interest in lowering his or her cost or adding to your order, maybe he or she can guarantee a better rate next time you make an order with their company! Work with whomever you like, but the bottom line is the price. Keep your product as cheap as you can without lowering the quality so your profit can be higher. With any company, it has jobs ahead of yours, so make arrangements for a production date because if you get orders from a retailer, you may have only thirty days to ship your order, and this can cause a lot of stress waiting. If that's the case, try to let the retailer know what position you are in, that you don't have that many in inventory and you will have to remanufacture more of your product, indicating you will need extra production time.

Producing Your Product With Manufacturers

So, ask for an additional thirty days or whatever reasonable amount of time you can agree upon. Make sure you get a purchase order with the shipping due date on it. This date will make the anxiety from producing on a deadline a little less stressful. When searching for manufacturers to produce your product, look locally. It will make it much easier on you if you are close to where your product is being produced. If you are not, look in *The Thomas Register*; this is the bible for entrepreneurs. It lists every kind of product and manufacturer, everything you need as an inventor. (Check for the toll free 800 numbers and save some money on phone calls). Most all libraries carry *The Thomas Register,* but if you do not have access to a library, many small manufacturing companies carry these directories. If you do not have access to either, you can go online. They have a great website, and its very easy to use: **www.thomasnet.com**.

The entrepreneur who has created a great new product has a problem that must be dealt with individually; that is, it is hard to figure out whether you should produce your product then seek out buyers or seek out buyers then produce your product. It is a question I battle with every time I create a product, but I always come to the same conclusion. Create a proto-type product first! If it is simple to produce and does not take a lot of funds, (this includes patents, trademarks and copyrights. Whatever it takes to protect my creation), then I will create it. (The number of products I produce for inventory is determined by the amount of funds left over after expenses protecting it). If it takes a lot of funds, I safeguard my creation and search for Investors. To start your business, you may have to go in debt in hopes that it will pay off in the future. If you cannot afford to go in debt, take your prototype, protect your creation, and go search for investors. Your prototype can also be manufactured using CAD (Computer-Aided Design). Your idea can be created using state of the art technology into a 3D virtual prototype.

Producing Your Product With Manufacturers

Or create the real thing: A working, fully functional prototype. Again, all these will depend on how deep your pockets go. The price can range from you creating your own virtual website (cost is up to you), describing and showing your invention without a product or another company producing your website and costing around two to three thousand dollars with a 3D virtual environment, to having a manufacturing company create a fully functioning model for a prospective company to see, handle, and understand your invention which will cost around six-thousand dollars, depending upon the complexity of your product. Then if you want a legitimate company to handle your representation and exposure, you can tack on a twenty-five percent royalty charge. There are justifiable reasons to manufacture your product. One is to sell to the general public, another is to target distributors.

When targeting distributors to sell and distribute your product, they can then see you have a working model and that the manufacturer will be able to produce it without having to wait on product prototype setup time. They also do not have to sub out manufacturing your creation and can order directly through you, simplifying the process for them. Then with a finished product you also have the option of seeking out companies for a marketing/license agreement in hopes they retain rights to manufacturer and/or sell your invention to their buyers. You can also seek out and hire a licensing agent who specializes in your type of product. Fees should be under one-thousand dollars. Never seek out a manufacturer or a licensing agent without first filing a Provisional Patent where your product can be viewed as "patent pending," and even then do not disclose your idea without a non-disclosure agreement. Just talk in general terms like, "I have a product that will solve a specific problem in a area you are familiar with," and hopefully it will peak their curiosity enough that you can set up a meeting. If you are unable to locate a specific licensing agent, then seek out a general licensing agent.

Producing Your Product With Manufacturers

Having a manufacturer create a fully functioning model for a prospective company to see, handle and understand your invention is what I recommend. Nothing gets across your idea to potential buyers of your product more than being able to hold, play, kick, punch, throw or utilize your product the way it's intended. This inventor's story will help you understand what I am trying to get across: creating the real thing, a working, fully functional prototype. Jim Kesler, the inventor of PRO WASHERS, an outdoor yard game his family played for decades, says, "I was a foreman for a molding company when I first came up with a new design for an old product. The product was a game that many people designed themselves. This activity was patterned after horseshoes but on a different level using washers and usually the owner shaped the objects out of wood. Hence, all games playing pieces were different, giving the advantage to the maker of the game.

I simply designed the game with every piece having the same shape and form out of plastic, giving everyone the same advantage. I approached the owner of the company at Mac Molding where I worked, and he agreed to do all the molding at cost. Then I partnered with the owner of LP Tool & Die who helped me with the design of the molding. This allowed me to still work at my job and run my business at the same time. After the molds were completed, I started with a provisional patent which through an attorney cost around four hundred and fifty dollars. (The cost is four times less if you do it yourself). From there I filed and received a trademark for "PRO WASHERS." Then my attorney filed for a design and utility patent, which cost around five thousand dollars. After we got our first good sample from the moldings and our provisional patent application filed, I started hitting stores within my hometown. I found the key to selling my product was talking to the right people: the buyers. I think sales representatives are good, but they don't know or care as much about your product as you do.

Producing Your Product With Manufacturers

Working diligently over the next couple of months, I got my product in over one-hundred small local stores. Then I found out about WAL*MART's local purchase program. To do this, my product had to be approved by the store manager and the district manager. Then it went to Bentonville, Arkansas, (where Sam Walton opened his first store) and buyers meet for final approval. After my product was on the shelves, I showed through sales graphs that my "PRO WASHERS" sold more than another popular outdoor game, horseshoes. I went from selling my product in eighteen WAL*MART stores in a few months, to nation-wide sales with WAL*MART in less than a year. What I believed helped me along the way with the buyers was my sales graphs. Showing them my sales on paper in black and white made their decision easier."

Jim added, "During that time while I was marketing "PRO WASHERS" under patent pending, I received approval for a design and utility patent completing my long accomplished dream." Jim was one in a million that was accepted by WAL*MART. Now his product is carried in over 3,000 stores throughout the U.S., and his story is one that all inventors can take to heart. Just getting that far would be a dream come true for most of us, and with his type of determination and commitment, we can make it happen too. If you would like more information on Mr. Kesler's family yard game, "PRO WASHERS," go online and visit his website at **www.prowashers.com**. Jim Kesler produced his product with these companies, and maybe they can help you with your tool, die, and molding needs for your invention.

LP Tool & Die Company
12808 Gravois Road
St. Louis, MO 63127

Phone: 1-314-842-3422

Mac Molding
12814 Gravois Road
St. Louis, MO 63127

Phone: 1-314-849-0646

Chapter Ten
Marketing

Marketing is defined as getting the product from the producer or creator to the consumer. Making people aware of the product, marketing can take on many functions: Buying, Selling, Storing Goods, Shipping, Pricing, and Financing, Entrepreneurial Risk and Marketing Information, such as studies of the market on your product, like who will buy them: Man, Woman or Child and what age groups, et cetera will find an interest in your product. To make our marketing plan simple, we will just talk about a basic plan of survival. We do not need to get deeply involved into how the big corporations do things because they do not pertain to us. They do things on a much bigger scale.

We need a small scale plan, so we can get set up and started today and get the goods from the maker to the market as soon as possible. We need to have a marketing plan made up before we ever have our product produced because it may cost us more than we can sell it for. Let's find out! We need a marketing plan and a product. Let's use your product or my *Beach Ball* as an example, and let's start production at ten-thousand. The product: *the worlds finest Beach Ball.* (If you have more than one item, such as a *Beach Ball* and a hair dryer, then you will have to have a separate marketing plan for each because of cost and sale strategies). Now, we need to break down the costs for our *Beach Ball,* and if you see anything that's left out when it comes to cost, make sure you add it in.

Marketing

A. Manufacturing Costs: This is the very bottom line, the cheapest you can have a *Beach Ball* made for.
   Manufacturing Costs = $2.50
B. + Expenses: Everything it takes to produce the item after manufacturing costs:
a) Costs of shipping from manufacturer.
b) Rent of office space or storage building, or both.
c) Utilities: telephone, electric, et cetera.
d) Packaging, shipping costs.
e) Advertisement/Marketing.
Expenses: $10,000. (Divided by 10,000 *Beach Balls* equals $1.00).

Expense Cost =	**$1.00**
Sub Total =	**$3.50** (Manufacturing and expense costs).
Sales (Commission) 10% =	**.35**
Subtotal Wholesale Cost =	**$3.85**

    Profit: Make this reasonable, because sometimes during the sales life of your *Beach Ball*, you may have to cut costs, and this is where it will come from.

	$3.85
Profit (your companies profit)	**$1.00**
Add .10 profit for the unknown	**.10**
Total Wholesale Cost to Buyer	**$4.95**
Suggested Retail Cost	**$9.95**

(Retail cost is the cost the buyers will sell your product for, which is almost always at least 100% markup from wholesale). You can give them only a suggested retail price because they may want to sell your product for more or less the going rate. That rate may depend on a lot of different things, like the clientele of the store and the volume customers buy your product at. Still, you must maintain some control over your product, so you don't end up in a retail price war. This may be why you would like to use a suggested retail price range, ($9.95 to $12.95) so a retailer can market to their clientele without being drastically undercut by another retailer who sells your product.

Marketing

Check the market you are entering: in this case, beach suppliers who will mark up your product from wholesale 100%. Depending on the market you are entering, the percentage markups will vary, such as food, which is very low, and high tech items, which may be very high, so call on retailers to get retail percentage markups in your product area. Now, let's get to the bottom line.

Profit: $11,000

This is the total profit for 10,000 beach balls at $1.10 each from total wholesale cost. Always do this because this is where your incentive for sales will come from, YOUR PROFIT!

Product:	Beach Ball......
Manufacturing Cost:	$2.50............
Expenses:	$1.35............
Profit:	$1.10............
Wholesale Cost:	**$4.95** (to retail buyer)
Retail Markup:	100% (approximately)
Retail Cost:	**$9.95**

(Suggested Retail)   **$9.95-$12.95**

This is a small breakdown that you can use with your product. You do not need an elaborate accountant breakdown. Keep it simple! You want to be able to keep your own records, so you can judge how your operation is doing. You will be the one in the beginning keeping track of all your expenses and profits, so don't over complicate things. All you need are basic accounting skills that keep track of your costs, expenses, and profits. Make sure you understand basic accounting because you will need your records at the end of the year to show a profit or loss from your business for tax purposes. You will use form Schedule C (Sole Proprietorship). Joint Ventures, et cetera, will use Form1065 or 1065-B.

Marketing

C. Promotional Advertising Strategy:

1) Paid Advertisement.
2) Free Advertisement.
3) Internet/Website Advertisement.

Now that we have completed the cost breakdown of our product, which is very essential to our marketing application, this gives us a basic foundation as to where to start. For the most part, we have to do a cost breakdown, so we can see how much we can spend on marketing. These marketing costs include advertisement, sales commissions, or salaries and expenses related to sales, such as transportation, et cetera. We can keep some of these costs low by marketing our product with free publicity. See chapter thirteen under "Free Publicity!"

D. Buyers:

This is a list of ideas where we might sell our Beach Ball.
1) Stores.
2) Conventions.
3) Mail Order/Mail Order Online.
4) Personal (one on one).

E. Sales People:

1) Yourself: (that's right, you will probably be the best sales person for your product, because you will have the desire to make it successful!)

2) A Sales Team: you can create a sales team without a lot of expenses by hiring sales people on commissions. It won't matter how many you hire, because it's not going to cost you anymore for one sales representative than for one thousand because they work on commission, which is already accounted for under expenses. But you may want to give them separate territories, so you don't have different sales people knocking on the same doors.

Marketing

3) Distributors: They make commissions from selling several different companies, products. (Essentially, everyone who works with you or for you will be in marketing positions. They are the ones the customer or buyer will be dealing with, and they will be the ones from whom they will form an opinion of your company and its products. So make sure the distributors represent you well!)

4) Buyers: They must be found by divisions. If you're selling *Beach Balls* and you want to find a buyer for one of the large department stores, like Sears/K-Mart or Wal*Mart, you can call one of your local stores and ask for the Sports Section. Talk with the manager in that section and ask him or her if their division is the one that handles beach balls. If not, get connected with the right division.

When you get the right division, ask the sales person for the company's main office where the buyers do all the buying for your particular product. When you get the phone number, also ask this sales person for the name of the buyer for that particular department; this gives you an advantage so when you call you can ask for the buyer by his or her designation. When the company operator answers, ask for the buyer by name, and ask if that particular buyer has an extension number or a direct line. Then the next time you call in, you can be connected directly without ever going through the operator and maybe even bypass the secretary. Normally, when you ask for a buyer by extension, operators won't question who's calling because they believe you are calling from within the company. Don't waste the buyer's time with a new product trying to sell him or her over the phone. The quickest way to get a buyer's attention for your product is to be brief. Tell the buyer your name, the company you are with, and a little bit of information about your product. Then you can ask the buyer what the company's address is so you can send him or her a sample and some information.

Marketing

Then say, "Thank you," and get off the phone. Send the buyer a sample and some information on your product, and on the mailing package, put the company name, then the buyer's name, so the buyer will get it directly. If you do not hear from the buyer within a week or two, you can follow up with a telephone call and ask the buyer if he or she received your product and what he or she thought. Now you are dealing with the buyer directly, and if this product doesn't go over, maybe the next one will; and you now have a buyer to contact personally. Do not contact buyers, publicize, or try to sell your product before it has been created. This will only end in frustration for the buyers because as time goes by, waiting for you to produce your product, they will lose interest. Finish the product, and then go to market. I lost thousands of dollars on one of my best creations because I had shown a prototype of my creation to two major gift store buyers before Christmas. They both liked it and made two very large orders.

I made orders through the manufacturers and parts houses to fulfill my obligation, but, because I had the parts shipped from (overseas) Hong Kong by a cargo ship, it took 60 days plus a couple of weeks for customs and another 30 days to complete a finished product. It was the middle of January before I was ready to ship, and every week I was getting calls from the buyers asking questions about their shipment. It was past the peak buying season for Christmas when they notified me that they would not be needing my product. I almost had a heart attack, and I negotiated with both companies to take partial shipments. I consider myself very lucky because I broke even. This is what I mean about trying to sell your product before you are ready for market; it could mean a fast end to a fast start. Do not let buyers know of your product unless you are willing to make them understand that you cannot produce your product on short notice. Be honest and maybe they will give you an order date you both can agree upon.

Marketing

Have the buyer write up a purchase order with a shipping date you both can be comfortable with, so trying to meet a deadline doesn't cause you to have a nervous breakdown. Marketing your invention yourself without using the "middle man or middle woman" will make for far better results than using a company that is allegedly in the business of marketing for inventors. Its primary concern is collecting money from unsuspecting, trusting individuals who look for outside help in marketing. These companies provide NO results. When your patent is approved and published in the "Official Gazette," you will begin receiving telephone calls and letters from these marketing companies. Beware! Beware! Beware! Get exposure for your invention through direct mail to companies who may have an interest in your product. Prepare a list of contacts, create a marketing brochure or post card (post cards are good because they don't have to open an envelope) that at first glance will attract attention, and send it to the "decision makers" of the company.

Wait a sufficient amount of time, and then follow up with a phone call. You can market your invention through syndicated newspapers or, better yet, to corporate business men and women who read informative marketing publications such as "The Wall Street Journal." If you are advertising for the sale of your invention and a prospective party becomes interested, you negotiate and agree on terms. It is quite simple. You have a contract written up; you review it, agree on it, sign it, and boom! You're a Millionaire! (Hopefully!) But if you negotiate for a licensing agreement, you need to have knowledge of exclusive and nonexclusive agreements. An exclusive agreement gives the licensee exclusive rights to your product for a certain amount of time agreed upon and pays you either royalties, a lump sum or both. A nonexclusive agreement allows you to license your product to more than one licensee. Either way, have an attorney review any contract before signing.

Marketing

There are four key elements every marketing program contains:

- Products (your invention) and or services provided.
- Promotions for your product or service.
- Distribution of your invention (product).
- Pricing of your invention (product).

Inventors usually have limited resources to expend on marketing, so concentrate on target marketing. Identify the people most likely to buy your product. The more profits earned on smaller volume of sales is better than less profit earned on the maximum number of sales, that is, if you can generate more money from a smaller amount of sales (maybe because your target market group is little green male aliens), than generating more volume sales at a lower profit (from all gender of aliens). It's best to make the most profit with the least amount of work.

Identify your target market and get the most return on your investment. Good telephone advertising is important and direct mail can be rewarding. The right price for your creation is important. The higher the price the lower the volume in sales. The lower the price the higher volume in sales. As an inventor, usually we target a specific group that needs our invention, so we can usually demand more for our product. You will need to test the market and decide on the best retail price and audit your products performance every so often and see if you need to change your sales strategy and pricing. If you have a low traffic location you will have to spend more on advertising. To succeed, the inventor must attract and retain a customer base. This will be trial and error. From large corporations to small businesses, they all work through trial and error. Although the larger corporations have a larger bank account to work with, they still have the same imminent fear of failure. Test market the need for your product, its buyers, and its cost.

Marketing

When it comes to marketing, the search for different types of marketing tools, strategies and ideas to sell and promote your products can be endless. So, maybe reinvent your thinking when it comes to marketing strategies and different ways to get your product to market, like one woman did with re:invention, inc.. Kirsten Osolind is CEO of re:invention, inc., a marketing company for women-led businesses. Re:invention's nationwide team now includes nearly 40 women marketing associates. As CEO, Kirsten brings over 14 years of marketing experience in leadership roles with Fortune 500 companies. Re:invention offers custom-tailored marketing programs and a website to fit the needs of women entrepreneurs. "We're on a mission to build more women-led million dollar businesses, with marketing strategy, promotions, and national public relations programs that deliver measurable results."

Kirsten says, "re:invention helps women get noticed, build credibility, and best the Big Boys. We've worked with some of the nation's premiere women entrepreneurs and their companies to help them achieve their goals and grow." Re:invention's blog -- the #1 ranked blog for women entrepreneurs -- is a toolbox for women entrepreneurs. With smart women quotes, breaking news, partner discounts, web polls and re:invention's Shoe of the Week, re:invention's blog inspires, amuses, and above all, educates. Each Saturday, re:invention presents *10 Tips for 10 Million Women*™, featuring a woman entrepreneur and her personal 10 tips for success. Kirsten goes on to explain; "It's a powerful example of 'women helping women win.' Our blog is a toolbox for women entrepreneurs with practical business and marketing ideas you can use today to turn your million dollar dream into a profitable and actionable reality." This is what marketing is all about. Find a niche, create a product or business, market it, and profit from it. If you're a woman entrepreneur and you want help or information, visit her site: **www.reinventioninc.com**

Chapter Eleven
Internet Marketing
& Sales

If your in business, you must market on the internet! If not, you will miss prospective sales. Over six million small businesses are connected to the internet and almost half have websites. The number of web sites double every six months. That means your competition is doing it. So you better be doing it! What's great about internet marketing is it makes no difference where your business is located. Your business is in every city, every country, every home with a computer throughout the world. As the company salesperson you can be sitting in Miami, Florida one second and knocking on someone's (web) address in Hong Kong, China the next.

Never before was it possible to reach so many people so fast before the internet. So you must create a *website*. To do this, you first must secure a *internet domain name*. Hopefully you will be able to secure the name of your business, like one entrepreneur did with **www.springbreakinc.com**; this internet domain name will be associated with this business owner throughout it's life on the internet, and so will yours. So make it creative and easy to remember. This is the name your customers will type in the web address box of their internet service provider. The cost is very reasonable and there are several internet domain name register services to choose from like **www.register.com** or **www.godaddy.com**.

While you cannot anticipate all the different types of domain names your domain name may be associated with, you may want to buy a few that may be similar to yours. Like if it's a case of possibly misspelling your domain name such as; "inventorfreehelp.com" or "inventorsfreehelp.com," buy both. Many of these register domain companies also give you free website design pages that you can select from. That is, they host your website for free. (If you create your own website, you will pay a monthly hosting fee). They will house and maintain your files on their server. In general, you rent space on a computer other than yours, and they hold your website. So, if you use the free hosting programs, you don't have to be a computer whiz or even understand HTML. *(Hyper-Text Markup Language)*. The authoring language used to create documents on the World Wide Web, HTML defines the structure and layout of a web site page by using a variety of attributes and tags.

But with these free simple to use page layouts from your domain manager, you just pick and choose, and before you know it, you have a website, sometimes in less than 30 minutes. If you design your own website there are certain things you should keep in mind. Don't use a lot of high-resolution graphics, not all visitors that visit your site will have a fast internet connection, and if takes a long time for your page to load, your visitors will become bored and leave. Try to keep your website confined to one page that is viewed at once rather than having to scroll down for a full view. Not everyone has a 21 inch monitor. Use colors and fonts sparingly. Sans Serif fonts are the best because they are easier to read. Ok, we have our domain name and website up, so now we need to attract customers. When a potential buyer is looking for a product like ours, he or she types into a search bar and hundreds of products or businesses that carry products like ours pop up. These are called search engines and if we want to get our product into the sight of potential buyers, then we need to get our product into these search engines.

Internet Marketing & Sales

Almost 80% of web users find the products or sites they are looking for using search engines such as Google and Yahoo. To get your company or product listed near the top of these search engines is a another thing, and maintaining a listing at the top can be very tricky. If you write and create your own website using HTML, you will use hidden codes within your web pages called metatags. The normal internet surfer does not see these codes on your web page, but most search engines using spider programs do. When they eventually run across your site, they read these metatags and catalogue your site into its indexes. Like I said, most all search engines track for metatags, but not all. It is not a requirement to use the metatags, but it can be helpful; once your webpage is operational (and I mean fully operational, don't throw up a trial page) with or without these hidden codes in your website, *register your URL* with as many search engines as you can, then their spider programs will look and ultimately find your site and index it.

This builds traffic to your website and that's our goal, bringing the customers into the shop. Now even though you are listed with a search engine, this does not mean you will be seen in the first 3 listings or even the first 50 listings. So, here is another way to move up the listing ladder on a search engine. It's called pay per click. *Pay Per Click Advertising* (PPC) is one type of online advertising that you pay for each time a visitor clicks on your advertisement and visits your website. You only pay when a web searcher actually clicks on a link and visits your site. How do you get these? You have to bid on a specific keyword. Let's say your website sells strawberries. You sign up on a pay per click search engine and bid on the keyword strawberry. Unfortunately, if other people have bid on the same keyword and out bid you using higher bids, then you will be listed in order of the highest bidder. Say, one bidder was $.09 cents and the other bidder was $.10 cents and you bid $.08 cents, your listing under the word strawberry will be third.

Internet Marketing & Sales

Every time a web searcher visits that search engine, types in the keyword strawberry, and clicks on your listing, you will be charged $.08 cents. Generally speaking, the advertiser that bids the highest amount on a specific keyword will show up #1 on that search engine listing. PPC advertising cannot be ignored. This is probably the cheapest, quickest, most effective means to link potential buyers to your site. Another good internet marketing technique is to create a banner. A *banner* is a graphic that you showcase on someone else's website, and when interested parties click on it, they are brought to your site. With compression software you can create your own banner or go online and find pre-made website banners for your site and others. You can host a *message board* where customers can interact with each other, leave comments or ask questions. There was a time when you had to pay someone to create a message board for you, but now you can find them free online.

These message boards make a great addition to your website. Check out **www.blogger.com**, its message board is free and is user friendly. If you are going to be selling products on your website, you will need a *shopping cart*. This allows customers to shop and order online. Along with a shopping cart, your site must be security compliant to protect your customers from identity theft when shopping at your website. This is called SSL (*secure socket layer*) and is a cryptographic protocol that provides secure communications over the internet. This certificate lets your customers know that their information, such as their credit card number is passing through a secured connection from them to you. The industry standard is 128 bit encrypted technology. There are several online companies available who sell both their shopping cart software and their secure services together. There are very few internet orders that don't accept credit cards, so you will need a merchant account. If a customer has to send a money order or a check he will most likely change his mind and search elsewhere for a product like yours.

Internet Marketing & Sales

Ok, that about sets up our online business. Let's move on to internet marketing techniques to drive consumers to our site using our web address. There are several things we can do:

- Create a link in your email back to your website.
- Get your website listed with the Chamber of Commerce.
- Include your website/email address in all your advertisements.
- Include your website/email address on all your business cards.
- Include your website/email address on all your stationary.
- Include your website/email address in all your press releases.
- Build an email database from customers visiting your site.
- Discuss your product in chat rooms, and leave your website address.
- Find media sites and leave product and website information.

As you become familiar with marketing over the internet, you will become more creative and find many ways of promoting your products and your company. View and learn from your competitors' websites and keep updating and adding new features to yours. Revise your "META tags." Run Promotions. Run Specials. Give discounts. Link up with other websites and their products, collect royalties from the sales of their products, and offer the same to them on your products. Keep in mind, as an inventor, you may want to use your website, not for sales of your creation but viewing your invention for licensing purposes, by showing a 3D vision of your innovation to perspective buyers or manufactures you invite to your site. Instead of setting up personal interviews with these buyers, you can send a description of your product along with your website address (where they can view your invention) by e-mail to virtually anyone in the world. If you have a product that doesn't need all the bells and whistles to show its value, just scan a picture of your invention into your site. The future of wholesale/retail businesses and products is the internet, so keep current with the changes and keep promoting your business and updating your website.

Internet Marketing & Sales

Domain names for your business or service can be bought for possible future use. I currently hold approximately 20 domain names for websites I have created or may create in the future. I do this because it is very hard to come up with a mark that will be suited for a business venture I may establish at a later time on the internet, say, two years from now. During that time period, anyone can have the same idea and register that same domain name. Then I would have to go back into the think tank and come up with another creative name, especially if I want a dot com domain name. I prefer dot com domain names, because people have become accustomed to that extension. But if you cannot register a dot com there are other options available such as; .net, .us, .org, .biz, .info, .tv, .ws, .cc, .pro, et cetera. The price is around $35.00 a year for .com domain names and may be more for other specific extensions like .pro which is used exclusively for medical doctors, attorneys, and CPA's and cost's around $350.00 per year.

- www.inventorsfreehelp.com
- www.inventorfreehelp.com
- www.inventorsUSA.com
- www.moonbritches.com
- www.actortalentsearch.com
- www.modeltalentsearch.com
- www.movietalentsearch.com
- www.musictalentsearch.com
- www.sportstalentsearch.com

www.siriusstock.com
www.votemayor.com
www.beachmayor.com
www.xmstock.com
www.xmstockholder.com
www.springbreakinc.com
www.alienbugremover.com
www.siriusstockholder.com
www.navarrebeachmayor.com

Several more are not listed. I may drop or keep these domain sites at my discretion. If I decide to drop one, I forfeit my right to that domain name. If you already own a domain name, you may want to look into registering your name with the USPTO. (Under trademarks). Federal law "grants trademark protection only to marks that are used to identify and to distinguish goods or services in commerce." If this applies, you apply for federal protection.

 *Chapter Twelve*
Selling

People spend millions of dollars everyday on products, and these products get to the market by sales people. We not only want to be the creator of these items, but we also want to be the sales person. Why? Because that's where the money is! That's where the satisfaction is! There's a great sense of self-worth when you sell your product because you know other people enjoy your creation just as much as you do. If you have never sold before, then you don't know where to begin; you're nervous; you're scared of rejection. Well, get over it! Those products all got to market by someone just like you; at one time, these professionals were you. No one will ever know about your creation unless you sell your creation.

The more you sell, the more you make, and before long, you are writing your own book and helping others do the same. If you have a product that you believe in, sooner or later you will find someone who believes in it too. Your customers are going to be concerned about the price and quality of your product, so make sure you are happy with it, so you will feel self-assured when speaking to others about it. Leave enough room in the wholesale price to negotiate. Ninety percent of the time, the customer always wants a deal. One way to determine sales of a product is to look at products that are associated with yours and see how your competition markets it, how much they sell it for and where and whom they sell it to. These other companies sometimes spend thousands of dollars in studies.

Selling

Save some money; follow your competitors' patterns. Check out your competition. If you are selling surfboards, get surfboard magazines. If you are selling clothing, get listings of clothing stores, et cetera. This type of research is critical because in the first stages of selling, you want to feel as confident as possible, and the more you learn about your product, the more confident you will feel when trying to sell it. One reason amateurs get so nervous in sales is that they don't know enough about the market they are selling in. One way to feel secure is to be knowledgeable about your product and its market. To find the right market for your creation, whether it be stores, catalogs, flea markets, whatever, narrow down the most likely buyers of your products, rather than trying to sell surfboards to golf stores or retirement homes.

Trying to sell your product to the wrong market is a sure-fire way to become uninterested in your creation because, if you are selling to the wrong demographics, no one will have any use for your product, and you will feel your product is useless rather than useful. So, do your homework, and, after you feel knowledgeable enough about your invention, your next step is to contact buyers. We can do this two ways: by sending out information to possible buyers and soliciting buyers in person. Let's start out with sending product information to the buyers first. It won't be such a shock, like a face to face meeting, and it will allow us to get to know our buyers before we meet them. This will lessen the anxiety. Make a small list of stores that meet your product's salability needs, and then call or write to these stores requesting brochures and catalogs. When you receive this material, check out the prices, the products, and the type of customers that frequent the stores. This will give you an edge when writing your sales letter. When writing to these businesses, try to tie your product in with the store's merchandise. For example: if the store features environmental products, create environmental sales brochures.

Selling

When dealing with large stores, buyers are separated into departments such as auto, furniture, toys, et cetera, so you must write to the purchasing department of that store. Describe your product in the letter and ask for the buyer's name, address, and, phone number in that department. In even larger stores, the buyers can be in one central location, or they could be split up by specific territories, like the Southeast. The more information you gather about your buyers, the easier it will be to win them over. Knowing your client, your customers, and your product, will make you a better sales person. The more you learn, the better a sales person you will become, and the more you will sell! Everywhere you go, talk about your product: when you talk with your friends, when you go to the grocery store, social gatherings, or even night clubs you might frequent, whenever and wherever you get the opportunity.

You never know who you might talk to that could bring sales your way. Anytime you take a vacation or go out of town, talk with someone about your creation. No one will ever know about your product unless you say something. If it is a product that can be sold in gift stores, plan to visit these stores while you are in the area. Look in the phone books; write down a list of stores that may be interested in purchasing your item, and call them to set up appointments. Make sure you are able to meet with the owner or buyer, or you will just be wasting your time talking to a salesperson who can only relay what you said, and this relation usually never results in a sale. Call all your relatives and family members. Send them information and samples if possible. Let them try to sell your product in their area. Give them ideas on how they can help you. Sometimes your relatives are good sales people because they speak not only of the product, but also of how they are related to the inventor. This will give the buyers a good reference to base their buying decision on. Selling to mail order catalogs is another option. Look for these catalogs; get the phone number off the inside cover; then call.

Selling

Ask for the buyer; explain your product; and offer to send a free sample with your literature and price list. Make sure the buyer is interested first because if he or she is not, you could spend a lot of time and money on mailing free samples. You can attend conventions related to your product and lease a booth for a couple of days during one of the many product display extravaganzas. The convention promoters will require a deposit or payment before the show, so make sure you get this information ahead of time because it does take planning. Example: If it's a boat product, attend a boat show; call ahead and try to reserve a booth. If the show is a yearly event, the earlier you make arrangements, the better. You select a booth on a first come, first serve basis. There are also several overlooked shops that could include potential buyers; one is Hotel and Motel gift shops if your product is of that nature. Restaurants, cruise ships, hospitals, are other possibilities.

I have even seen some entrepreneurs set up booths inside famous name franchises and sell their products. You can purchase mailing lists of mail order companies that sell products like yours and even businesses that may be attracted to your creation. Create your own mailing list from these sources. Find out the name of the buyer whenever possible and mail it to his or her attention. In your letter, request a response (R.S.V.P.). When surveyed, the buyers stated that they would rather see the sales material directed to them personally. There are advertisement and printing companies that can do a great job with a post card. They show a picture of your product on the front and a description of your product on the back. Whether it be your business or your invention that you want to publicize, all these companies need is a photograph and your sales material. This is one way to capture potential buyers. It's relatively a low cost with a lot of impact. You can mail these completed post cards out with a return request for buyers to respond if they would like to see a sample of the product.

Selling

As a sales person, one of the advantages to selling your product is sometimes having the promotional material or gimmick to go on along with your creation. These could be items such as a display that attracts attention to your product or a give away item with the sale of your product. Sometimes, the buyers know what they want for their stores and what would help to move your product. Offer to work with them in whatever way it takes to sell! If confronting department store buyers, make an appointment by telephone or go there during buying hours. Time is important to the buyer, so don't waste it. Make your sales pitch in a business-like manner. Take suggestions openly, and agree on terms. (Usually payment in thirty to sixty days from the day your shipment arrives is not uncommon). Try to leave with some sort of a signed commitment. Make sure you can produce your product in large quantities; if not, stay with the small gift stores. They buy in smaller quantities and are usually sole proprietorships where the owner is also the manager.

The owner/manager can make a buying decision immediately without having to confer with a board of decision makers. During your sales meetings, sometimes a buyer will request to take your product on consignment. That is, the buyer does not buy the item, but offers to put it in his store, or stores, and, when the item sells, he pays you a percentage of the sale and he or she keeps a percentage of the profit. I do not recommend consignment for someone who has a creation that is manufactured by the hundreds or thousands because there will come a time when you will not be able to keep up with your consignment sales. In my case, for example, when I created "Bankruptcy!" the board game, I was having trouble with sales. I was in the knowledge process of everything, from learning how to sell to department stores, to making out receipts, to practicing my sales pitches. I wasn't doing so well when a small local gift store owner mentioned he would take my game "Bankruptcy!" on consignment.

Selling

I thought that was as good as a sale, so every time I failed to take an order, I offered the owners consignment. I would leave approximately five to ten games each time. That was a mistake I didn't recover from. Not so much monetarily, but mentally. I still do not remember all the stores I left the games at or how many

games I left. With a new creation, you have to start getting your product in the consumers' sight somehow, and if consignment is the only way, then it's the right way. Just keep track of where you leave your product and how many you leave, and, don't leave too many on consignment because keeping track will be a problem along with collecting sales.

The whole problem was not just keeping track of where I left them, or how many, but driving back to the stores where I did remember I left them, and asking the owners how many were sold, and having to continually collect my sales profits. This became such a burden that I just ended up leaving them with the stores and never collected. It was costing me more in time and money than I would ever regain in profits. A little helpful hint to make sales happen faster is if you must resort to leaving your product on consignment, take out an ad in a local newspaper with the buyer splitting the cost of the ad.

Selling

Give his store top billing in the ad with a headline, but feature your product with a large picture. This way, your consignment product will sell faster, and when the store sells out, you can make a cash sale to the buyer next time. I cannot teach you how to sell, and I cannot make you a successful salesperson. Sales are made on a individual basis, and the only method is the school of hard knocks. You just keep knocking on doors and knocking on doors until someone says, "come in." A splendid way to test a new product line is with online e-commerce auction sites (like eBay).

There you can set up an e-commerce site without having the expense of setting up a site of your own. There you can test market your product with sales from other people bidding on your item. This has created a whole new wave of entrepreneurs, and as with any new venture whether you are creating a storefront online or meeting a potential buyer face to face, take the time to prepare. If meeting a potential buyer, practice in front of a partner or mirror. You will learn as you go along, but along the way, don't let friends or associates get the best of you. This happens way too often; your friends and relatives find out you have a great product, and they want it for free.

Selling

Before you know it, you have given away fifty free samples. Learn from me. I wouldn't even give my mother a free "Bankruptcy!" game. (LOL). I made her buy it! Read all the books you can; talk to all the sales people you can. You need to get every bit of information that will help you sell your creation, but the bottom line is you have to sell it yourself! Somewhere in the beginning, no one knew anything about sales, about invoices, about shipping and receiving costs, or about wholesale and retail costs. People learned as they went along, and this is what you have to do. You just have to get out there and do it! Don't wait for someone to motivate you or sell your product for you because no one else will have the same enthusiasm you have. You will be your own best sales person. Don't wait for buyers to call in with orders for your product.

It's not going to happen, and you won't sell your product if no one knows about it. You have to be the one who announces it to the world. You can read and study all the latest in selling techniques, but if you don't apply them, you will never know your potential or your products potential. Do not be afraid of disappointment. Sales are full of despair, but you progress through each day on the hopes of success. You must recover immediately from rejection. Keep your self-esteem high. Success can be yours, but it doesn't come easy; it's full of a lot of hard work. That's why there are sales people because not everyone can take the hard work and rejection, but you as the inventor must in order to create sales and fulfill your dream, your dream of selling a successful product!

Chapter Thirteen
Free Publicity

After you have created and protected your idea, an important step is to let the public know about your product. You could run ads, run promotions, sell on radio or TV, rent an airplane and tow a banner, lease a billboard, or hire a movie star. There are hundreds of ways to promote your product, and there are hundreds of ways to lose hundreds of dollars! But there are also ways you may be able to do these same things without costing you any money. How! Free publicity! Newspapers need stories to sell newspapers, and your new creation is just that, news! Start with your local, hometown newspaper. It will be more receptive to your story because everyone locally may be able to relate to you, and that sells more newspapers.

Call and ask for a section writer or editor in the field of your creation. For example: If your creation is a new style hat, then you ask to speak to a fashion writer, not necessarily the fashion editor because he or she is usually too busy, and the fashion writer can relay your story to the editor when the time is right. If all else fails, though, speak to the fashion editor if you cannot get through to the writer, explaining your new creation and how it's going to change the world. Make it new, exciting, and most of all, make it news! After you convince the writer to run the story, then convince the writer that the newspaper will need pictures for the story showing different people wearing your hats.

Free Publicity

After you convince them to take the pictures, stress that it would be even better if the pictures could be run in color. If you have convinced the paper to run the story, you may want to bring the color picture idea up to the writers when you meet to discuss the article. It all depends on how confident you feel with the writer at the time of your phone conversation or interview. If this calling of reporters doesn't go over on the first try, there are still several things you can do. Have your friends start calling in telling the editors how great your creation is and what a fine article it would make for their newspaper. I didn't have any friends I wanted to trust with my publicity secrets, so I called the newspaper, disguised my voice, used a fake name, and talked up my product. I would do this a couple of times a week with different writers until I found one willing to convince the editor to write a story. Another trick is to contact another section in the paper such as the Money section.

Convince the money section writer that this story has to do with the executive and stock brokers who wear hats on Wall Street and that you are going to change the image of these executives and stock brokers with your hat. Keep at the writers in different sections of the newspaper until you hit on someone who is interested in your story. Use holidays as an attraction for your product. If it's St. Patrick's Day, color it green and associate it with the holiday. If not your product, maybe dress the product's user green or color the product's user green. For example, maybe you have a special cat collar that locates your cat when he or she strays off. Tell the writer that your cat always strays off on St. Patrick's Day so you are coloring your cat green with a special safe non-toxic dye and putting on this special collar so you can locate your pet easily. Then offer to color other pet owner's cats green for free if they come by your place of business. If it's Valentines Day, show how couples using your product have fell in love and rekindled their relationship because of it. Always make it <u>news</u>worthy.

Free Publicity

Another great trick after you convince the editor to write the story is to tell the writer that this would make for a great syndicated story. See if he or she can convince the editor to put it over the wire. (The information highway for newspapers). Have the writer talk with someone from the (AP) Associated Press or the (UPI) United Press International to carry your story. Then other newspapers throughout the country that have to fill space in certain sections of their newspaper may run your article, and that's nationwide advertising for free. The cost of this would be astronomical if you had to pay for that kind of space in that many newspapers. That's not all. Every time you go out of town, call local newspaper reporters and ask if they would like to run a news story on you and your product while you are visiting. If you live away from where you grew up, your hometown newspaper may be interested in running an article on you.

Even your old high school or college newspaper may run an article on one of their alumni that has created something of interest. Everywhere you go, plug your creation. It won't cost you any money, and with all the publicity you get from these articles around the country, it may even make you a few bucks. If phone conversations aren't your thing, then you can make up a Press Release to send out to newspapers and publications. This is just a simple letter about your product which gives the writers some information on your creation. Make it informative and as interesting as possible, but do not make it commercial. That is, do not over stress your company, location, prices, et cetera like an advertisement. The newspapers want news, not advertisements, unless you are paying for them. Put your name at the top with whom to contact for more information. This concept may be a little easier for the first time entrepreneur because you will be able to reach more newspapers by mail than by phone. You could also add you would be willing to run an advertisement on your product the day your story runs.

Free Publicity

It may also be cheaper writing to newspapers, but I believe the results are actually better speaking to the reporters by phone or in person. You could also use them together for more attention. Try a phone call, and then send a news release. Use all your weapons. These techniques can also be used for radio and television although, for the most part, these media rely on spontaneity. You can create publicity by promoting your product in a way that draws attention. If your product relates to a certain crowd, say for example, a *Beach Ball*, then bring it to the beach and take pictures showing sun worshippers using it on the first warm day of summer. Throw several of your beach balls into a crowd at a rock concert or a local dance club. Relate your product to the public where it will create controversy. Magazines that relate to your product could use your creation for a story in a feature article. Contact magazines that write stories on entrepreneurs or that write stories for the public's curiosity and reading pleasure like airline magazines or your local city magazines.

There are many publications that could use your story. You may even be surprised how interested magazine writers are in your creation. That's because writing is their job, and they need stories to keep their job. Your product may not be an invention, it may be a book or a song, and the writer that wants to do a story on you may be in a different part of the country. In this case you will have a long distance phone interview and you will need to provide your own picture for the story. So, have a professional good quality photo of yourself on hand to mail out. Always tell the truth about whatever questions the reporter asks. If the reporter asks a question you can't answer, tell him or her so, but offer to get the answer as quickly as possible. Don't try to cover up with anything other than the truth. They're reporters; if they find out you weren't telling the truth or the information you gave them is wrong, they may not print the article or, even worse, they may print it to discredit you.

Free Publicity

Never tell a reporter anything "off the record" because there is no such thing to a reporter. Anything spoken to a reporter is considered part of the investigative research, and if it makes for a more informative article, it will be printed. Never give an answer such as "no comment." The reporter takes this as an insult. If the reporters are there to write a story, then give them a story. If you cannot comment on that particular question, then give the reporter an answer as to why you cannot comment on that particular question. Maybe it's not your field of expertise. If not, give them the name of someone who can answer that question. To feel more comfortable with the news media, have someone you know pretend to be a reporter, and have this person ask you questions so you will not be nervous at the time of the interview and you can feel more confident about the questions you may be asked.

Don't answer any more than the question asked, but do write down for yourself information that you want to get across, and somewhere in the interview, bring it up. I sometimes write out a list of comments that I would like the public to know about my product or my company. I glance at them often, and when the time is right, I bring them up. At the end of the conversation, I ask if the reporter would like to keep this list as a reference for the story, and the reporter always takes it because it helps him or her write the article. So do your research, and when the article comes out, you will be very proud. I always had copies of the articles that were written on my products, and I would add them to the customer's shopping bag. Publicity that you did not buy gives you and your product credibility. A high profile way of getting free publicity is to donate your time and/or your product to an organization that is planning a charity event. On a bigger scale, you could plan your own event such as a battle of the bands, dance, or a 5k fun run. Even something simple like a car wash or bake sale with all proceeds going to the charity of your choice can be beneficial.

Free Publicity

Pick a church or a charitable organization such as The Ronald McDonald House or The American Cancer Society, et cetera. These organizations are more than willing to help you promote your event on their behalf. Not only do you promote your event and your product, but you promote goodwill as well. You will want to create fliers to announce this extravaganza, and when you do, put your company or personal name on them. There is a lot of free advertisement through these types of charity events including newspapers, radio, and television. You will be recruiting many sponsors and, for their contribution, they will want  to be recognized throughout the event with brochures and media exposure. You are also a sponsor by providing your time and effort to make this event a success, so promote your event and yourself.

The television and radio stations have an allotted amount of free time per day, and newspapers save space for charitable and community service announcements where you can send in a press release announcing your upcoming event for approval and scheduling. This time is for P.S.A.'s (public service announcements), and it is free of charge to help promote any event where contributions go to a charitable organization. Usually two months in advance is not too early, so plan ahead. After approval by the radio station, this publicity will be announced throughout the day every day and will start about two weeks before your event. Your press release will want to carry an important message announcing this charity event. Examples for press releases that can be beneficial to your company may go like this:

DANCE

**A Street Dance will be held this weekend
in front of the Vic-Vincent Game Company with all proceeds going to
"The Children's Hospital."
For more information call this radio station or
"The Vic-Vincent Game Company."**

Free Publicity

Free publicity can be approached in a number of different ways. One of those ways is an indirect approach, and by this example, you will understand what I mean. One of my selling techniques, no matter how little in sales it produced, produced publicity; and who knows how many sales at a later date were because of this gimmick being in print. The gimmick is to place an ad in the lost and found of your local newspaper. This will produce only publicity at first and maybe profits later, but it will not be any loss, even if sales do not increase because most newspapers will carry lost and found ads for free. It can read: Found Bankruptcy Board game. Call 000-0000. This is an indirect approach, as is placing ads in certain publications. These require no direct sales and make it easy for the beginner sales person. You could also use this same technique to draw attention to your company such as "Found: a set of keys in front of The Vic-Vincent Corporation. Call 000-0000." These concepts are mostly just thoughts that you can put to use with your ideas.

Of course, no one can claim them and no sales will be made directly, but the price of publicity was worth it because it was FREE! I once traded with a flower shop to promote a sun-tanning/bikini business I co-owned. They would bring fresh sunflowers to my business with their business cards, I would promote their flower shop and in turn, they would promote my business in their shop with brochures and business cards. Every week the flowers were free, and so was the promotion. Promotions can call attention to your business or products such as putting up signs like Michael Jordon buys his clothes here or Jennifer Lopez will be here Wednesday night (of course these people are not the real celebrities, they are just ordinary people with the same names). These types of promotions can backfire, so be careful. You can also transfer an interesting news release about helicopters, for example, by offering free helicopter rides at Vic-Vincent's Game Company on April 1st. (April Fools Day).

Free Publicity

In this case, I would switch a real helicopter for a children's amusement ride helicopter. (The kind found in front of discount stores that you put a quarter in for a ride). Another way that publicity can be approached is attention. How many times have you seen the local exterminator drive around in a VW automobile that looks like a huge mouse or insect, or an ambulance used as a means of transportation for the Rug Doctor? I have even seen a Cadillac Eldorado that looked like a chicken for a chicken business. These are all ways that you can attract attention to your product or business. These types of movable signs can be used in highly visible traffic areas, or if they are not appropriate, you can use a truck. Erect two opposite facing signs in the truck bed, secure it well, and park it. You can paint the side of a van or your company vehicle in a way that attracts attention, add your company name and phone number on it, and while you're at it, if you want to look larger than you are, you can also paint Company Vehicle #6 on the back.

Vic-Vincent is shown here inside this helicopter which is just one of a variety of products he promoted under an international marketing company he named: Access International.

Free Publicity

Now you have six trucks. Sort of. Sometimes, even just the color of a vehicle will draw attention to you or your product. Try to associate your product or business to your gimmick. This will give it more visibility and marketing potential. Rent a party boat or barge and erect a sign. Then sit it out in the water to advertise your business or product. Use the snow and some food coloring, and in a visible area, create your own sign. Make up some T-shirts with your company or product name, and add a catchy phrase or picture to get attention. Make up fliers and put them on cars. Pass them out in an area that would attract customers. Anytime you sell an item, stuff the shopping bag with a flier with news of your creation and how people can save and buy more of your product. Have coupons printed that can save customers money on their next purchase, or special coupons that can give two buyers a discount when they buy together. Your invention is news. If not news to the general public, maybe it's news to the people in the field of your invention.

Vic-Vincent is shown here inside one of the first electric/solar cars he sold in the United States under Solar Car Corporation.

Free Publicity

Let's say you invented a new bike. There are several trade journals or newspapers that write for just companies and businesses involved in the bike trade. These journals update businesses to new technology, new materials and machines, almost anything the bike business will find as useful information to help their companies. If, for instance, you cannot find a certain trade journal for your product, look in *The Working Press of the Nation*. This directory lists thousands of magazine, newspaper, radio and TV stations you can contact for information. To keep in circulation, all of them need stories like yours. Magazines are a little tougher to get into, but it doesn't mean it can't happen. I and my creations have been written about in *Inc. and Success Magazine.* It took several calls and letters, but persistence paid off. I was able to get the editor's attention by writing several short letters and enclosing my already publicized invention articles from several newspapers. (I believed this helped a lot because these articles gave me clout).

Look on the inside covers of magazines, publications, and directories; go to book stores; take down the names of writers, and write to them. If your story is of any interest to the readers of their publications, they will contact the editor who will give his or her OK. Then the writer will contact you for more information. Be prepared. Always have a script sheet with information about your creation beside the phone, so, in case a writer from the magazine calls, you won't be caught off guard. This way, you can refer to the script sheet when asked questions because when you are caught off guard, you could say all the wrong things and regret it later. Be prepared. The internet is a massive field of free marketing. Create your own website, link up with other websites, send out an immense email campaign. Market your product to other website wholesale/retail distributors. Do you know radio stations in America need thousands of guests per day to meet the needs of the public listening audience. Radio interviews cost you nothing.

Free Publicity

You can do an interview for radio anytime or anywhere now with cellular phones. Even from your home in your favorite lounge chair. If you had to pay for a big syndicated radio station advertisement, the cost could be as much as one-thousand dollars per <u>minute</u> and on well known radio celebrity shows, ten times that amount. You can be an expert or controversial subject for a radio show that normally runs for one hour. That's many thousands of dollars saved and maybe many earned from pitching your product while on the show. Once you have completed one show, start working on the next, take the radio circuit till it dies out. Interviews on radio will make your product sales rise.

Here are a few publicity tips:

- On your website place your picture and contact information. Many writers and reporters search websites for stories.
- Try to create controversy. Nobody wants to listen to a boring story especially on radio.
- Send news releases.
- Start a news letter from your website.
- Offer free advice.
- Call the newspapers with ideas or take fascinating pictures using your invention or product and send them to the newsroom.
- Get in online chat rooms and talk about your products or website.
- Start your own TV show on a public access channel.
- Write how to articles for newspapers, trade pubs and magazines.
- Get on a speaking, radio or TV circuit.

Creator of "BANKRUPTCY!" the board game.

# Chapter Fourteen
Toys, Games
and Gimmicks

This chapter covers a question that people ask me a lot. That is, how do you create a toy, a game, or some kind of a gimmick? In these next few pages, I will explain how I did it. I want to stress that I generalize on these topics, trying to give you the most information possible from my experiences. I want you also to understand that there are no certain guidelines to success, but maybe you will have a better chance of survival following my failures and successes with certain products I have produced and marketed. Many entrepreneurs and inventors create ideas for toys, games, and gimmicks but do not know where to turn for information on how to create and produce their creations.

This section should lead you in the right direction. Before you dive into dark waters, you must evaluate your finances and personal surroundings by asking yourself a number of questions. Will you or your family suffer from this project? Can you afford the time and money involved? Are you highly motivated? Can you face rejection? These are just a few of the questions you must answer before you decide to create your idea because creating your idea not only requires hard work, money, and determination, but it requires a risk as well. If you decide that it's worth the risk, then your next step is to produce your product, game, or gimmick.

Toys, Games and Gimmicks

You start by drawing a design of your idea. You don't need professional drafting tools for this; use what's available in your home. Use different size drinking glasses for circles, a book edge or ruler for lines, rub off letters for words, et cetera. Your design does not have to be perfect to create a working model. You will change your design many times before you are satisfied with the way it works and looks. Use what you can find for the time being. If you need playing pieces for a game, look in your home for small items like sewing thimbles or in the garage for nuts and bolts; use whatever works. If you're building a toy or gimmick, the same applies; for now, you just want to produce a rough prototype. Be cost effective in the beginning. After you produce this rough prototype of your product and you believe you have created something unique, then start searching for manufactured parts and their prices to produce a more improved prototype for production.

Research using your library again, for references of manufacturers of these parts look in *The Thomas Register*, or go online to **www.thomasnet.com**. (For parts made of plastic for instance, search under plastics, game parts, or toy components. For parts made of metal, look under steel or aluminum). Check directories like plastic technology magazines. Look at the advertisements. Call these different companies and get as many quotes as possible. If they do not have what you are looking for, ask them to refer you to another company. If no one has what you are looking for, you may have to have a custom made mold manufactured of your artifact to produce it. There are many companies that do this. These companies are under the headings plastics, molds or metal/plastic molders. There are many types of molds and many different molding processes such as extrusion, injection, blow, rotational and thermoforming. When you have all these price quotes of your separate parts, add up the total cost. This will give you a rough estimate of what it will cost to produce your prototype.

Toys, Games and Gimmicks

Then get quotes from the manufacturers to produce your product from one, to one hundred, to five hundred, to one thousand, to five thousand, et cetera. After you have collected your price quotes, pick a quantity you can afford to have manufactured and do a marketing plan. You can then decide whether to have a manufacturer produce your idea or put your money into one good prototype for presentations and search for an investor or produce the product in a profitable number and sell it yourself. Yourself! That's right, think of the possibility of buying all the parts and assembling the product in your living room yourself. That's what I did after I received the quotes from a couple of game manufacturers. I decided I couldn't afford to have someone else produce the board game "Bankruptcy!" so I located all the parts, bought them, assembled them, and packaged them in my living room, myself. So, don't give up. If you can't afford to have someone else produce it, do it yourself! If you want it bad enough, you will find a way.

Before you make a decision like this, to do it yourself, make sure you have enough room to store and assemble these parts. If not, rent a humidity controlled storage unit or small office space. Use a garage or attic if you don't need air conditioning. In determining your manufacturing cost for a board game, you will need estimates for a gameboard, paper money, spinners, playing pieces, instruction booklets, et cetera. Have a small print shop print up the instructions,  playing cards, et cetera separately along with the play money, or you can save money by having the instructions and rules printed on the inside cover of the box by the box manufacturer.

Toys, Games and Gimmicks

If you have created a stuffed animal or doll, you will need items such as the eyes, hair, nose, voice chips, et cetera. Then you must sew and assemble. Look for these items in craft stores. Craft stores carry many items that can get you started on almost any idea. When you find something in a store that may be useful in creating your product, look on the back of the package for a company name. Then call them for a wholesale catalog and price sheet if you plan to manufacture the product yourself. That way you can order direct from the factory. This will save you money. Always buy wholesale when possible, especially if you are ordering in large quantities. The more you order, the cheaper the cost per item. After you decide whether or not to produce your product yourself or have a manufacturer create it for you, you will now have to create the packaging. This is probably the most important part in selling your product because this is what the buying public will see before they ever touch your product, and if it is not eye-appealing, they may never see it.

Your packaging draws attention to your product; that is how you sell it. When you walk through a store of packaged items, the colors, the pictures, the words, they all draw your attention to the product. That is what you want your package to do. The same thing that draws your attention to their product is the same thing you want to do to draw attention to your product. So walk the aisles of toy and gift stores, and create an eye-catching package. How do you create the package? Well, you draw a picture of all the sides to a box or package on paper. Each square represents a side of the box. Measure your product from the top, bottom, front, back, and its two sides. Allow enough room for packaging material if needed such as bubble wrap or packing paper so your product does not get damaged. In the case of a game, you most likely will not need packing material, so create your box snugly.

Toys, Games and Gimmicks

Use other game or gimmick boxes as a pattern. If you are unsure, take or mail your prototype to a box manufacturer; he or she can cut out a sample pattern to fit your product for you. They will also color print your box when you have it produced. I won't hold to the idea a prettier package sells with many different colors, because my product, "The Decision Maker" sold very well in just two colors with a photograph on the front, and the image was a black  and white photo. In this case, the name and picture drew the buyers' attention, not the color package although created; with just two colors and black lettering, it looked very good. (Silver and burgundy).

I got this color scheme from looking at other packaged products in the store and those colors caught my eye, so I used them. I bet I  saved a lot of money because some large corporation probably spent thousands of marketing dollars on testing those color schemes to sell their products. You can pick your colors, draw your illustrations and design your box on your computer, or you can take it to a professional typesetter/illustrator who can do the job for you. This typesetter/ graphic artist can give you lettering to design your box or gameboard of all the words, phrases, and logos on a special gloss paper that you can paste-up with a glue stick. Then you can move your inscriptions around while you are designing and creating your product. If you are creating a gameboard, use an old gameboard you have around the house. Trace out the pattern of squares.

After that, cover your playing board in white poster-board and trace your squares onto this new board or create your own new map pattern that the players can follow. This will give you an idea of dimensions and overall looks that you can now start designing. Design your board game for playing; then add your

paste-up art and words. Use your computer word processor; pick your font, font size and style of characters. Paste them on your playing cards or board spaces for a more professional look.

Color in where needed with markers. It will soon all fall into place. If you use flip-over playing cards in your game, use business cards and turn them over on the white side and write or paste-up your instructions on them. You need not go too far in making this game design perfect because that is what you will be paying an illustrator to do. The illustrator/graphic artist will make a perfect copy from your rough

illustration and paste-up art work, photo/color separation ready for the printer. When this is complete, take it to a printer or the box manufacturer who can create color film negatives of your box

and/or gameboard, assuming that your box is not printed in black and white. This is called a "four color separation."

Toys, Games and Gimmicks

These color separations are what the printer uses to print your box, et cetera. For each color you add, the cost will increase and you will have to have another negative. Keep in mind the cost in printing one, two, three or four colors, and a glossy finish may make the difference when it comes to drawing the buyers' attention. Also ask for a "color key"; this is a final look of your color design before printing. The color separation method is one way printers can produce your design. Another way is the newer faster computer printing software method. When you visit your printer, visit their shop and look over their equipment. When a printer meets your approval and your display box is complete, you are now ready for the final touch, shrink wrap. If you plan to assemble this game, toy, or gimmick yourself and are in no hurry, then buy a roll of shrink wrap with a heat wand for cutting and a heat gun (or hair dryer) for shrinking the film. If you are in a hurry, then buy the more expensive type that seals and shrinks your box automatically.

Look for the manufacturers of heat shrinking suppliers under packaging machinery. Explaining shrink wrapping is not the same as seeing it done. If possible, visit the manufacturer. If not get brochures with prices and instructions; if you still do not understand how it works, then visit a video/movie rental location. These places usually have one to repackage videos that people return. A gift shop has one to shrink wrap specialty items like gift baskets. Shrink wrapping is the most enjoyable part of the process, "the final touch." As stated in previous chapters, get protection. You may need patents, trademarks, and/or copyrights. Most toy or game companies will not accept your product without them. Over five-thousand products in the toy industry are introduced each year, and there are close to nine-hundred toy manufacturers in the U.S. alone. These companies themselves employ a great number of people to design and produce new games, gimmicks and toys every year, so they are for the most part uninterested in your product.

Toys, Games and Gimmicks

They pay their employees large amounts of money to create these types of products, and if just one of them has an idea similar to yours, they could face a possibility of a lawsuit for infringement. They do this because it's cheaper for them to pay toy and game designers from eight to five than to pay you royalties. (Royalties are a percentage of an item's gross sales). So, they do not welcome any outside creations contrary to what you have heard. If one of the company staff members has created an idea similar to the one you submitted, then there could be a conflict as to who created it first, and to avoid all that, they just do not accept outside ideas. With all this competition plus the other odd-million just like you, I hope that your product is one of a kind. With all the rivalry, you are going to have to make a name for yourself. So, how are you going to make a name for yourself and get the big name companies to notice you? By sales! That's how. You must get their attention by selling oodles of whatever it is you have designed.

After you have sold a couple of thousand or obtained a big order for your product, then write the toy, game or gimmick companies. Tell them how well you are doing, and ask if they may be interested in buying the rights to your product or signing a licensing agreement. But for no reason take your product off the market. I lost a lot of momentum banking on a investor buying the rights to "BANKRUPTCY." This investor ask me to take it off the market while we negotiated so as to not lose future sales to his company. I agreed while we negotiated for over one year. Then negotiations failed. I received nothing and I lost almost two years in sales and publicity. It was more then three years before I could recoup from that loss and disappointment. All in all, in the industry, you have a couple of options; either you can sell your prototype to a toy or game manufacturer, create and sell it yourself, or have someone sell your product for you, a middleman or woman who will broker your product and negotiate for you.

Toys, Games and Gimmicks

They are referred to as "Toy Brokers" or "Agents." They work on commission and sometimes royalties. Located in the yellow pages under "Toy Consultants" or "Agents," these Agents may be able to get inside by using their contacts in places you could not even get through the front door. One reason you would not have a chance is again the possibility of an infringement lawsuit. The "Agents" are trusted by those companies. Again, do not be discouraged. Seek out smaller manufacturers. These companies may be more receptive to your idea. To keep from being disappointed, seek out the manufacturer that represents your type of product. If you have a board game, seek game manufacturers, not model car manufacturers. You can cut down on the disappointments by making a list of these manufacturers, calling them, and asking them if they accept outside ideas. If they do, ask who the person is you can write or speak to about your product, and, if you speak to this person, use the same telephone approach from the chapters on "Marketing" and "Selling."

If you do or do not speak with anyone, send just a letter, videotape, photo, CD or computer disc with pictures and information about your product before you send out a sample. If you are able to meet with an interested party, make sure you have this representative sign one of your disclosure forms. If you are lucky enough to get a licensing agreement, the usual royalties are from 2-10% of the gross sales, unless you had a broker negotiate for you. Then you will have to give up a percentage of the royalty to the broker. Exhibit your product at a trade show or place your own ad in a game magazine or newspaper. If someone or some company wants to represent you and requests money in advance, BEWARE, BEWARE. It's most likely all they want is your money. Keep in mind when creating a product to sell to the public, safety is a concern. There are federal regulations you must comply with, especially for children under the age of three.

Toys, Games and Gimmicks

You may obtain a copy of the government regulation ASTM F:963 and the government's regulations from the American Society for Testing and Materials. I created "The Sticky Ticky," a small toy bug that stuck to the skin of children. I even spent quite a bit of money producing it but when I went to test market it, (which I strongly recommend you do with your product), I found the first thing small children did was put it in their mouths.

This scared me enough to pull the whole project. I was afraid a

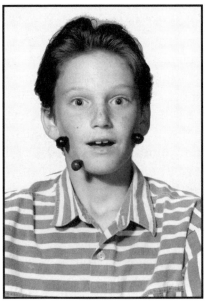

small child might choke on one. I could have gone to market by complying with the federal regulations, but it wasn't worth the risk. Making it in the toy and game industry is very tough; you have many competitors. Not only do you have the big manufacturers in the U.S., you have foreign manufacturers importing into this country to deal with, plus the small independent manufactures and the many people like yourself. But with hard work, determination, and a good product, you can be one in a million and make a million!

Toys, Games and Gimmicks

High tech games. Game development. Programming. It's the future. The old school of board games is becoming extinct. If you want to get into creating games for now and in the future, you will need to learn coding fast, the basics of code looping, et cetera. There are many sites for beginners on the internet. Some do a great job of explaining programming techniques to the novice. For those that already have a knowledge of programming, there are many, many sites for you. There are forums and chat rooms that you can enter and share your knowledge with others. You can discuss the problems you are having with a certain design feature in your game and find a solution through networking with other game designers. Some have professionals that give advice. There are two excellent websites for game developers. The first is **www.gamemaker.nl** where, if you are totally clueless, you can create a game without writing a single line of code. You can do anything you want with the games you produce from their codes, you can even sell them.

The other site is **www.gamedev.net**; here if you're a little more experienced, they offer great information on designing computer games. There is also a couple of great articles for beginners under resources. Check them both out, and maybe I will soon be hearing about you and your new computer game! I personally do not know one creator of a interactive game that has been marketed, mostly because it takes many designers to create the games we now use on our home computers and game boxes. But you could be the first, and when it happens, I want you to e-mail me at this website: **www.inventorsfreehelp.com**, so I can finally say I know someone who did it. That would be so grand to be a creator of an interactive game. The future in gaming will depend on developers like you and others like you. I can speak for myself: I want more. I want better graphics. I want more realistic sound. I want 3D interactive games. I crave these games and can't get enough, and there are millions more like me.

Beware of Fraudulent Invention Companies!

Over the years, several unscrupulous companies have offered assistance to inventors in patenting, developing, and presenting the inventor's invention to the industry. As a result, many inventors have been taken advantage of.

RIPPED OFF!

These companies promise riches as far as the eye can see! They mislead you into thinking you have the best idea in the world if you only send an "up-front fee" for their services. If you read or hear about these organizations promising to help the inventor succeed in promoting their invention,

BE FOREWARNED.

The worthlessness of these companies and individuals has been investigated by the *Federal Trade Commission* and many have been shut-down. They soon open up again under different names and pretenses so be very leery when searching for investors. Do not fall victim to the marketing evaluation. This is almost always a

SCAM!

They will ask you to sign an agreement to represent you and to do a patent search to file for a patent on your invention, but they can not give you the results. Why? Because this could be practicing law without a license.

Never Send Money And Be Careful When Signing Anything!
Ask yourself this one question. If my idea is actually that good, then why do I need to pay these people? The answer is you don't. They should be paying you!

DO IT YOURSELF!

Chapter Fifteen
Scams

You have seen the slick inventor ads on TV, read them in magazines and heard them on radio. These are "hooks." You feed on the bait, and they reel you in. They send you their free "inventor's kit." Then they want upfront money right away to evaluate your invention. Then after the evaluation, they need more money for a report which comes in a nicely bound manuscript. This manuscript says your invention is patentable and marketable. Now you will need to send more money to continue the process of obtaining a patent on your invention and then more to market your invention. That's how it works. Thousands, I really mean thousands of inventors, like yourself are targeted by fraudulent invention promotion firms.

Some use different catch titles like "licensing and marketing," but they all have one thing in common: To take advantage of your enthusiasm, solicit you with exaggerated promises about the potential market success of your invention and take your money on a promise to obtain a patent. These are white collar thieves who for a large fee, provide you with a basic market research paper and a virtually worthless patent. I just can't stress enough to do all the research yourself. Don't rely on others to do it for you, and this will never happen to you. You can make your own decisions based upon what you have read and learned about protecting your invention, and if you use a licensed patent attorney, you can feel comfortable knowing you have the best protection possible.

Scams

But if you decide not to research the information yourself, and you think you found the right company to help you, here are a few questions to ask the firm HELPING YOU! Especially before you sign anything, get these answers in writing: **CAUTION**

- Do they have an upfront fee and if so, how much? What do I get for this fee?
- What is the total cost from the time of submission of my invention to obtaining a patent and a licensing agreement?
- What is the total number of customers who have received a net profit as a result of this companies promotional services?
- What is the total number of clients who have made more money than they have paid the company?
- How many companies have they been affiliated with in the last ten years?
- What other names have they used in the U.S.?
- What is the number of accepted clients? What is the number they rejected? (Valid companies only accept about 5% or less).
- Has the company ever been investigated by any agency?
- Can I get names, phone numbers, addresses and copies of contracts of former clients in my area?
- Who pays and picks the patent attorney to do a search and patent application?
- How many clients do they have and how many received licensing agreements? (If the percentage is lower than 5% hang up).

And if that's not enough, here are few more warning signs:

*They guarantee you a patent! <u>No one can guarantee a patent</u>!
*You are told your invention is sure to be a success! (They tell every one that).
*The sales person wants money upfront before they do anything.
*You can't reach a salesperson directly without leaving messages.

Scams

There are so many different scams that go on in the market place that could affect us (the inventor) and our business, that I couldn't name them all. Most of them now include the internet. There are "phishing" (fishing) scams. There are "Pay Per Click" scams. There are "You've got mail scams!" "You got pictures scams!" Welcome to E-Bay Fraud alert log-in scams and more! These are the Top Ten Online Scams released by the Federal Trade Commission:

1. Internet Auction Fraud Scams.
2. Internet Service Provider Scams.
3. Internet Web Design/Promotions (Web Cramming) Scams.
4. Internet Info & Adult Services-Credit Card Cramming Scams.
5. Multi-level Marketing/Pyramid Scams.
6. Business Opportunities and Work-At-Home Scams.
7. Investment Schemes and Get Rich-Quick Scams.
8. Travel/Vacation Fraud Scams.
9. Telephone/Pay-Per-Call Solicitation Fraud Scams.
10. Health Care Fraud Scams.

Why am I listing these? They have nothing to do with inventing. It seems that way, but when your on the internet trying to sell products, closing deals, visiting other sites for information, these type of scams are going to pop up in front of you and in your email. So if you are aware that these type of scams are out there, maybe I can help you avoid some serious trouble. Sometimes just opening these emails can wreak havoc in your computer. They can input worms that eat your hard drive information or other programs that can take important private information out. The internet has revolutionized the way we do business and gather information. If we want to continue using the world wide web we must constantly monitor and update with virus protection, pop-up blockers, et cetera and maintain a good backup program for our hard drive. (We do not want to lose our invention data that we saved to our computer).

Scams

Pay Per Click Scams: We talked about the good use of bringing pay per click customers to your website. Now I want to talk about a good thing that can go bad. There is evidence that some pay per click companies have used scammers to click away at your ad, paying them a cut of the profits made. They inflate traffic statistics to defraud advertisers. When you pay per click, these clicks add up! They have even designed automated programs called clickbots or hitbots that click on your advertisement for them. Click fraud could become rampant if it goes unchecked. It is sure to undermine the confidence of the unknowledgeable inventor that would like to use this program to bring customers to their site. Do your homework before you pick a Pay Per Click company. Ask around, talk to your friends that market over the internet. Get trusted advice.

Phishing Scams: Masquerade as official looking companies that send you email notices to encourage you to click on a link that takes you to a copycat website that looks identical to a company you are familiar with. Once you are there, they ask you to enter your username and password, sometimes even private information like your social security number, your credit card number and its expiration date. Once that is given, they may use your account to send spam. I know it happened to me. It was an online exact copy of my Internet Service Provider telling me I had received pictures. I put in my user name and password, but didn't get any pictures. A few days later, the ISP banned me from email. The fraudulent firm used my information and sent out thousands of spam letters. Not only was I scammed, I was embarrassed this could happen to me. I am so careful. But the scammers are very good at what they do. It's hard to keep up. One place to go to try and keep up with all the new online and offline scams is the Federal Trade Commission. They provide information and services that provide inventors and online businesses with cautions about new scams, providing (if you get scammed) a place to go to address your complaint.

Scams

Internet Pharming Scams: Pharming is a play on words for "phishing." It involves almost the same technique but with much worse consequences. Unlike phishing, where email users click on the links in their email and the user is taken to fake identical sites, pharming captures a user on the way to a credit card firm or bank. Pharming works by sending a virus-laden email that installs a small software program to the users own computer. When you go to your banks website, the program redirects you to a look-a-like website. Then it asks you to update your information such as PIN #'s, log on names and sometimes even drivers license numbers. What's alarming with this technique is that pharming can reroute thousands of internet users. With phishing, they scam one person at a time. Congress has introduced a bill that calls for prison time and fines, but don't depend on them. Watch your keystrokes.

Website Scams: If you plan on using the Web to create your site for potential buyers and investors, be cautious. There are some devious companies, claiming to provide free web services such as design and hosting, then billing them for services that were never authorized. The bogus charges usually appear on their phone bills or in a direct invoice. This is an illegal practice known as "cramming" or fraudulent invoices. I usually view my monthly phone bills and my invoices, but if you have someone else doing your accounting, you may never know you were being charged. If you get a phone call from a company like this offering you a free 30 day website, just hang up. Protect Your Company's Business; Know your rights. The law allows you to treat unordered services as a gift. If you receive bills for services you didn't order, don't pay.
- Review you phone bills. If you find an inaccuracy on your bill, follow the providers instructions on your statement.
- If you have employees, assign someone to document all purchases, and train your staff how to respond to telemarketers.
- Buy from people you know and trust. Be skeptical of cold calls.

Scams

Self Publishing: Vanity publishers produce around 6,000 titles each year. Under a typical arrangement, the author pays much more than the printing bill, receives 40 percent of the retail price of the books sold and 80 percent of the subsidiary rights, if sold. Many vanity publishers will charge you $10,000 to $30,000 to publish your book depending upon its length. It is hard to understand why an author would pay $30,000 when he or she can have the book printed for $1,500 or less. Vanity presses almost always accept a manuscript for publication and usually do so with a glowing review letter. They don't make any promises regarding sales, and usually the book sells fewer than 100 copies. The vanity publisher doesn't have to sell any books because the author has already paid him for his work. Therefore, subsidy publishers are interested in manufacturing the book only.

They are not concerned with editing, promotion, sales or distribution. The review copies a subsidy publisher sends to columnists usually go straight into the circular file. Reviewers are wary of vanity presses because they know that little attention was paid to the editing of the book. Further, they realize there will be little promotional effort and that the book will not be available to readers in the stores. Therefore, the name of the vanity publisher on the spine of the book is a kiss of death. There is a lot of money being made from unsuspecting authors. The vanity press is not a good choice. Do not pay a vanity publisher to publish your book. Self-publishing isn't new. In the early days of the U.S., the person who owned the printing press was often the author, publisher and printer. Some authors have elected to publish themselves after being turned down by regular publishers. However, many more have decided to go their own way from the beginning. Some have started as self-publishers and sold out, and some have built their own large publishing businesses. Like Dan Poynter, visit his website **www.parapub.com** for more information on self-publishing your book.

Scams

Invention Marketing Companies: This story comes from a very skeptical inventor. Everything he did to avoid being swindled by those idea/invention companies seemed to put him deeper into the development marketing scam. His name is George "Jake" Jaykus. Jake invented a tailgate table for pickups. He was exhilarated with the fact, that not only could he use this product, but thousands like him could do the same. With no idea where to start, he saw an advertisement on TV that gave him the incentive to move forward. So he called them. Here's his story. "I immediately called this company and talked with them about my product. They liked the idea and said they could help. First I would have to send approximately $500.00 to file a Disclosure Document, and they would also send me a marketing survey on my invention. I did that because they put the fear into me that someone would steal my idea. (**The Hook**). The next call was to further my protection with a patent. They had three different levels to choose from.

1. $9,995.00 plus they receive 10% of sales.
2. $8,500.00 plus they receive 15% of sales.
3. $7,500.00 plus they receive 20% of sales.

I chose the $7,500.00, but negotiated their percentage of sales down to 10%. I found investors who believed in my product, and I was able to raise the capital to move forward. But I was still skeptical about this company and wanted to make sure they were legit. So, I booked a flight and flew to Washington, D.C. to hand them over the money personally. When I arrived at their office, it was just how I pictured it in my mind. Secretaries, office representatives, computer specialists and drafting rooms. Not only that! They were just a few doors down from the USPTO. I thought to myself, no one would be that stupid to be breaking the law that close to a U.S. government office. They greeted me, showed me around and made me feel comfortable. So, I handed over my $7,500.00, (**The Sinker**) signed the contract and flew home.

Scams

The next time I heard from them about my product, I was told it was patent pending, and during the wait time, I could send out postcards to would be clients and manufacturers who may be interested in my tailgate table. So they sent me postage paid postcards, I addressed them and sent them out. As time went by I realized this list was a stalling attempt to deter me from calling my idea/invention representative to find out if he has set up any meetings or arranged any negotiations with potential buyers. They made it sound like they were going to do all the work for me. Many months went by and I finally received my patent. (It was a design patent). Now I thought I was on my way. I called and called and called for marketing help but no one would return my phone call. Months later this company went out of business and with them went my incentive to bring my dream to market. I became discouraged. Years went by and my product wasn't any closer than when I started. So I gave up.

It's now thirteen years later, and I am finally getting up the encouragement to bring my product back to life." I first met "Jake" at an inventors club meeting many years ago, where he told me and others about his new tailgate table that could be used at football tailgater parties, et cetera. He was excited, but that all soon changed. Now years later he is talking to inventors again but telling them a different story in hopes just one of them will listen and can avoid a similar fate. Are you listening! I hope so, we have discussed enough about this industry throughout this book. So I won't go into anymore detail about these firms but end this chapter with my thoughts. "It is sad in America where the inventor is truly the motivation of our country and the success of our nation that deviant people can prey on unsuspecting inventors and not only take their hard earned money, but take their motivation to succeed. I want you to succeed and so does this country. Our nation depends upon the inventors success. The world needs creations from our ideas. So, our Government designed some ways to protect us."

Scams

"The Law"
The American Inventors Protection Act of 1999

On November 29, 1999, Congress passed the AIPA, which for the first time imposed a duty on Invention Marketing Companies to disclose information to prospective clients before they sign contracts. Specifically, a company must disclose:

- Total number of inventions evaluated by the promoter in the past 5 years.
- The number of these inventions which received positive and negative evaluations.
- The number of customers who contracted with the promoter over the last 5 years.
- The total number of these customers who received a net financial profit as a direct result of the promotion services by the promoter.
- The total number of customers who have received license agreements for their inventions as a direct result of the promotion services by the promoter.
- The names and addresses of all previous invention promotion firms with which the invention promoter or its officers have been affiliated with over the last 10 years.

Any customer (inventor) who has contracted with a promoter and has been injured by an omission to state any of these facts, or any other material fact, or by any material false or misleading statement by the promoter will have a civil cause of action for actual damages or statutory damages of not over $5,000, plus costs and attorneys fees. If the court finds the promoter's actions to have been willful, taking other complaints into account, the damages may be trebled.

These provisions took effect on January 29, 2000.

Scam Assistance

If you still have questions there are many places to turn such as the Office of Independent Inventor Program at the USPTO.
Mail for <u>complaints about Invention Promoters</u> may be sent to:

Mail Stop 24
Director of the U.S. Patent and Trademark Office
P.O. Box 1450 Alexandria, VA 22313-1450
Telephone: 1-800-786-9199 Fax: 1-703-306-5570
E-mail: **independentinventor@uspto.gov**

You can file a complaint with the FTC (Federal Trade Commission). By contacting the Consumer Response Center by phone: 1-202-FTC-HELP (382-4357); TDD: 1-202-326-2502

By mail:
Consumer Response Center
Federal Trade Commission
Washington D.C. 20580
By e-mail visit their website.
www.ftc.gov

The Commission cannot resolve individual problems for consumers, but it can act against a company if it sees a pattern of possible law violations. The FTC is even tied in internationally to help prevent these deceptive practices from reaching our country, so if you have any information that could help other inventors anywhere in the world, please call them. You may also want to contact your local small businesses in your community to help local inventors avoid a similar fate if you have been scammed.

Several groups have formed an alliance in cooperation with the Small Business Administration (SBA) to help alleviate this problem. So, if you need help in a certain area call them.
1-800-827-5722

Chapter Sixteen
Depression and Inspiration

I have always thought someone needed to take the time out to write a section on depression. Everyone writes motivational stories, but what happens when you hit rock bottom? When you have spent all your time and money trying to make your business idea or creation a success? Your personal life has been shot; everyone considers you a failure, and you even start thinking, "maybe I am a failure." "Maybe this whole invention thing is a waste of time!" I have read several books, newsletters, business and financial magazines, and heard many motivational speeches for "entrepreneurs," but I have still not found one article or heard one speech on depression for these risk takers.

No one wants to talk about it; it's un-motivational, but I will because if you can't relate to failures, you can never be a success. Each day you may have setbacks. Some days you may have minor setbacks, and other days you may have major setbacks. With any luck, not many, but you will have them. This is a serious subject to those who have risked everything at least once on a dream to become famous and wealthy or just a little bit comfortable. Depression is going to happen to you sooner or later and may already have. You may be at that stage now. Everyone around you is criticizing everything you do; no one is being supportive; no one wants to give you any words of encouragement. What do you do? Well, I know what you do!

Depression and Inspiration

You look for someone else to motivate you, someone else who has a creative idea and is starting to market that idea or has been marketing his or her own business or products. This type of person can relate to what you are going through, and you can mentally rely on each other's support. All entrepreneurs hit bottom, but remember, that's the risk we took when we first started and said to ourselves, "I'm going to risk everything I have to try to make this a reality! I believe in what I am doing so much that I wouldn't be able to live with myself if I didn't try! I'm going to risk everything I own, and probably a lot I don't own!" You know what I'm talking about, Loans, Loans, Loans! Through each other, you can network with buyers, retailers, wholesalers, even customers. You can talk about things that worked for each other and things that didn't work.

You can feed off each other, generating excitement and motivating each other back to the point you were at when you started this whole crazy idea of becoming successful and independently wealthy. If you have not met someone like that, look in the newspapers; there are always articles on someone creating a new business or product. Join or start an inventor's club. (Visit, call or go online and search the SBA for the closest inventors club near you). Run ads looking for individuals like yourself. Read about entrepreneurs in the business section of your local newspaper. Some night clubs even hold business after hour get-togethers during the week: Like **Seville Quarter** in Pensacola, Florida. Have your local club do the same. Go to a Chamber meeting and converse with other business people in your area. These are all people who need to network, finding future business deals and clients. Motivational People! Stay away from non-supportive depressing people; depressed people won't accomplish much. There are plenty of support groups for these individuals, and you don't want to join that kind of support group! Being depressed is about the only time they're happy, and making someone else depressed makes them very happy!

Depression and Inspiration

I myself have failed on numerous occasions, and I do not consider myself a failure. What I would consider a failure is if I had never tried! I may not have become successful or wealthy, but I have become a success. During the course of my depression, I found two entrepreneurs who risked everything, even quit their jobs to pursue their dreams, and both were at rock bottom. (My advice is never quit your job until you are making more money than your job pays now). I felt pretty good around these two because they were worse off than I was, but they still offered words of encouragement, not discouragement, to me. They both had products to market and sell, and both had spent nearly every dime they had on their dreams and ideas. They were finding it hard enough to meet their own financial needs while still trying to support the success of their products, and in both cases, they could not maintain the expense of their product or their finances.

One had to file BANKRUPTCY! The other had to find a job and go back to work, but we all could relate to one another, talk about our problems, and network our sources. We all fed off one another's input, and in the case of the one who filed bankruptcy, he never stopped pursuing his idea. I found out he has done tremendous things with his product. His creation was in casual clothing wear for men and women for all seasons and all ages. He never gave up, even when he was filing for bankruptcy. He is an inspiration to all he meets and was a big help to me with personal and business problems when I was depressed. When I wrote earlier that all entrepreneurs will have this bout with depression, sure enough it happened to this same entrepreneur again, and I was there to motivate him. So networking with people like yourself is very beneficial, not only for business but also for personal problems because they both affect each other. It's very good therapy to network, and who knows, it may save you the cost of medical bills for the psychiatrist you may be needing, but couldn't afford! (LOL).

Depression and Inspiration

You become a failure only when you quit trying, so never give up. Take it to your grave, and at the least, you will have succeeded in proving you died trying, and that's something people will remember you for: The one who never quit. That's something people can relate to and dream about. Most people want to be just like you, but they are afraid to take the risk. That's what makes us special, different, but special. We are a breed who would rather risk it all to try to become successful than to be like all the rest and live a boring unproductive life. Inspiration comes from famous people who were labeled crazy for trying to create inventions like the airplane. These were people who had failure, after failure, after failure, and never gave up. Everyone called Da Vinci, Edison, even Columbus crazy. Maybe they were; maybe that's what it takes to get things accomplished: a driving desire to make it happen, no matter what people say about you or your ideas.

Think about the crazy Christopher Columbus, one of the really true hard-core entrepreneurs. He had to go to the Queen of Spain and convince her for three ships to sail around the world, a world she thought was flat. He had to sell her on an idea, a theory. That had to be one of the biggest gambles in history, and he did it! Not only did he accomplish attaining Venture Capital by speaking out on his belief, but when it was over, he also proved his theory was correct. His biggest reward had to be the feeling he got from proving to all those people who didn't believe in him that he was right. The world was round. There were a lot of people at that time with negative attitudes about his theory who tried to make him out as irrational, and not a soul would give him the slightest bit of financial or moral support. Moral support is very important to any entrepreneur. One of the reasons we strive for success is for recognition from others. (We love the attention!) Don't you think Columbus ran into a lot of personal and financial problems that made him depressed? How about Thomas Edison?

Depression and Inspiration

After his fifty-thousandth failure trying to find a new source of rubber in plant matter, a disheartened assistant said to him "We have made fifty-thousand experiments and we still have no results." "Results!" exclaimed Mr. Edison enthusiastically. "We have great results. We now know fifty-thousand things that won't work!" He never gave up. So get out of your chair and do something. You've got to make yourself famous. You've got to keep working at it daily, nightly, and in your sleep. Get out there and talk it up; no one is ever going to know about you or your ideas if you keep them to yourself. You must keep going from person to person until someone believes in you and your idea. Don't procrastinate. Procrastination is the downfall of many inventors and their ideas.

I would like to sum up this chapter with a poem written by a man who was imprisoned in bed with Lou Gehrig's disease, unable to move or make a sound. He wrote this poem with a computer by blinking his eye. This is the epitome of this chapter on depression and inspiration.

> Every morning in Africa, a gazelle wakes up.
> It knows that it must run faster than the fastest lion,
> Or it will be killed.
> Every morning in Africa, a lion wakes up.
> It knows that it must outrun the slowest gazelle,
> Or it will starve to death.
> It doesn't matter whether you're a lion or a gazelle,
> When the sun comes up in the morning,
> you'd better be running!   *Ed*

Stop reading books on how to be successful and go out there and become successful! Don't wait for something to happen. Make it happen! Make it happen today, not tomorrow. Go! Go! Go!

SUMMARY

From the time we are born, our surroundings have an effect on our lifestyle and our life. We can be born in poverty, handicapped, even just plain unlucky. We can accept the fact of our situation and continue on in this lifestyle or we can <u>choose</u> to change. To succeed, you must change whatever holds you back. Do a self evaluation. If you need money to make your invention a reality, then look at what your doing with your money. If you smoke, quit smoking; put that money away. If you spend a lot of time playing tennis or golf, spend less time. These are quick self satisfaction enjoyments you are going to have to do without if you want to become successful. You must concentrate on the future and look toward a lifetime of satisfaction. It sounds like very harsh advice, but self-made millionaires put all their hearts and souls into their dreams. Nothing stops them. They work at it 24 hours a day, yes even in their sleep.

$uccess is hard work. No one is going to give you anything. You have to work for it. Success will not come to you; you have to make it happen. Many successful people come from lives that are far much worse than yours. No matter how bad off you are, you will always see someone worse. So don't dwell on the fact that you will never make it because you have no support, no money, no talents, no skills, and you have no luck. You have no excuse! We have been given the ability to choose. If you can't make sacrifices to change your habits or your lifestyle, you may just be another person with a good idea.

"We may not be born with the ability to change, but we are born with the ability to choose."

"Make the right choice. I wish you success."

WEBSITE
INDEX

www.inventorsUSA.com

www.inventorsfreehelp.com

www.wini2.com

www.lawdepot.com

www,uscopyright.gov

www.taxi.com

www.fullsail.com

www.lawguru.com

www.ascap.com

www.bmi.com

www.sesac.com

www.harryfox.com

www.parapub.com

www.cafepress.com

www.springbreak.com

www.booksurge.com

www.loc.gov

www.isbn.org

www.uspto.gov

www.siriusstockholder.com

www.intelproplaw.com

www.bpmlegal.com

www.uschamber.com

www.score.org

www.sba.gov

www.irs.gov

www.business.gov

www.thomasnet.com

www.prowashers.com

www.reinventioninc.com

www.register.com

www.blogger.com

www.siriusstock.com

www.gamemaker.nl

www.gamedev.net

www.ftc.gov

www.sevillequarter.com

www.moonbritches.com

www.alienbugremover.com

www.nashvilleconnection.com

These website addresses are featured throughout this book. If you have purchased an online electronic copy, just click on one of the links above and go to your destination.
If you have any questions about anything you have read or anything as an inventor you need help with, visit my website.
www.InventorsFreeHelp.com

BOOK INDEX